GYPSY FOLK TALES

GYPSY FOLK TALES

Collected by John Sampson

With Engravings on Wood by Agnes Miller Parker

ROBINSON PUBLISHING

with

LONDON

ROBINSON PUBLISHING
with Breslich & Foss
11 Shepherd House
5 Shepherd Street
London W1Y 7LD

First published by The Gregynog Press 1933
as *XXI Welsh Gypsy Folk Tales*
Published by Robinson Publishing 1984
Illustrations © The Estate of Agnes Miller Parker
Series design: Lawrence & Gerry Design Group

ISBN 1 85004 021 4

Printed in Great Britain by
Richard Clay (The Chaucer Press) Ltd
Bungay
Suffolk

FOREWORD

THE twenty-one folk-tales contained in this volume have been chosen from a store of over fifty collected by the late Dr. John Sampson from the Gypsies of Wales. Recorded in one of the purest dialects of Europe, the stories lose much in translation and, in an English rendering, often fail to reflect the dignity and severe simplicity of the original tongue. For it is well-nigh impossible to reproduce in an uninflected vernacular the style of the folk-tale peculiar to every Gypsy idiom in Europe—a succession of short, crisp sentences, consisting sometimes of but a single word strongly accented: *ratí* night fell, *choianí* she was wroth, *chalé, kedé te chan* they ate, they made an end of eating. The Gypsy story-teller, with his flashing eye and dramatic gestures, his breathlessly interjected 'Lo!'s and 'Now's to introduce sentence after sentence and his sudden change of tense from historic past to vivid present, makes us feel that the incidents he relates are actually happening before our eyes.

This glamour necessarily disappears when the story, instead of being orally transmitted, is written down. If, therefore, some of our examples sound "stale, flat and unprofitable" in translation, I would ask the Reader to transport himself to a camp-fire or a barn in the heart of Wales where the tale was first told. Here on a dark night, or by the light of the moon, some ancient story-teller of the race of Abram Wood—possibly "Black Ellen", the Romani Shahrazad, herself—used to relate to a company of Gypsy men, women and children tales often long enough to occupy a whole night in the telling. Suddenly, to test the interest and wakefulness of her listeners she would interrupt her narrative to interpolate the meaningless exclamation *Tshiocha*

'Boots!'; and unless the sleepy boys and girls or their fathers and mothers immediately responded *Cholova* 'Stockings!', the tale would be broken off never to be resumed.

Faithfully reproduced in the words of the original raconteur, "in a form scarcely less fixed than the text of Holy Writ", these Welsh Gypsy stories have been handed down through the ages from grandam to grandchild. It was from Matthew Wood, who inherited this priceless treasure from his grandmother Ellen, a granddaughter of the patriarch Abram, that Dr. Sampson collected the bulk of his tales. They were taken down in such favourite haunts of the Gypsies as the banks of Tal-y-llyn lake or the river Alwen, the slopes of Foel Fawr above the tiny village of Abergynolwyn, the Bodynlliw woods on a spur of Bron Banog, or the cottage of Caegwyn and the village inns of Llandrillo and Bettws-Gwerfil-Goch. The Gypsy Matthew, in his prime a romantic figure with mystical deep-set eyes, aquiline nose, sensitive mouth and long black curls reaching to his shoulders, was a prince of story-tellers. In moments of emotion the Romani tale would come tumbling from his lips at a terrific speed almost too fast to be recorded, & Matthew, carried away by the drama he was relating, would often identify himself with the hero.

And a poor sort of hero this Gypsy *Jak* was. In Dr. Sampson's words: "Always the youngest brother and generally despised as a fool, he is cunning & fortunate rather than wise and deserving and, while possessed of courage, somewhat of a braggart and a liar. His virtues are reverence for his mother, generosity in sharing food with strangers and helpfulness to men or animals in distress. In love affairs, in spite of his uncouth manners and slovenly appearance he is always successful over his rivals, though more courted than himself a particularly ardent suitor."

The story-teller, however, cares naught for the morals of his characters. He may vary the title of the tale to suit his individual taste, preferring for instance 'The King of the Herrings' to 'The Beautiful Hill', but for better or for worse he gives us the text exactly as he heard it: even the local colour and picturesque detail with which the stuff of his story is embroidered has been inherited from his forbears. "A Gypsy narrative is naturally cast in terms of Gypsy life", says the folk-lorist; and so in the tales of Matthew and his son Harry we find such pleasant Gypsy touches as the fortune-telling and hedgehog-hunting episodes in 'The Eighteen Rabbits', the appproval of a barn's fitness as a lodging-place in 'The Little Crop-tailed Hen', the fear of police-inspection in 'The Man and Woman with too many Children' and the "good hedgehog's liver" demanded as a reward in the tag to that variant of 'Hänsel and Gretel'. "But", concludes Professor Halliday in the *Journal of the Gypsy Lore Society* where Dr. Sampson's Romani texts were first published, "I know of no story which can be called specifically a Gypsy story, and the repertoire of Gypsies appears to conform naturally enough to the land of their sojourn." So "in the dear lovely land of Wales", when *teulu Abram Wd* tell tales of Enchanted Castles, the Devil, Fiery Dragons and Fairy Brides, we breathe the atmosphere of the Welsh 'Plas' and the Welsh farm, find kings transformed into squires, meet constables and keepers as well as ogres in the forest, and recognize Arabian peris masquerading as "little women and little men beautifully dressed in the old-fashioned style".

And may this Romani description of the fairies—*ridilé raikanés ar'o phurikano drom*—be the verdict of posterity on the first Welsh edition of Dr. Sampson's Gypsy fairy-tales!

May 1, 1933.   D.E.Y.

CONTENTS

THE FIERY DRAGON.

THERE WAS ONCE A GREAT HALL, a squire, his wife and his daughter. And a poor man came there to ask for work. The old squire had a talk with him. "I have naught for thee to do," said he, "unless thou lookest after the cows." "Very well, sir." The squire went inside, and told the maids to give him something to eat. He got his bellyful. The old squire showed him where he was to sleep. And the poor fellow was happy. He went to bed. ⬫ In the morning he arose and went outside to wash himself. Now the young lady comes out to call him into the house to get his victuals. The young lady asks him whether he would like a drop of beer. "Yes, I will take a drop of beer." The lady packs the food and the beer in a wicker basket. ℭ Jack arose, took the basket, and set off. And the old squire was standing outside to tell him where to go with the cows. "There has been many a cowherd here before," said he, "who failed to bring back all the cows. One of them has always been stolen." ℭ Jack left him, and strolled down the fields driving the cows before him. He came to a pleasant little spot & there he put down his basket. While the cows were grazing in the meadow Jack sat down & smoked his pipe. It was a hot day. ℭ Suddenly a dwarf appears. "How art thou, Jack?" The dwarf sat down beside him, and they chatted. "Art thou hungry?" said Jack, "there is some food over there." The little old man ate his bellyful. Jack passed him the bottle that he might drink. "Jack," said the little old man, "when thou returnest, give this to the young lady." The old man gave him a beautiful plum. ℭ "Jack, dost thou see yon old castle?" "Yes," quoth Jack, "I see it." "Over yonder dwells a giant, and it is he who steals one cow every day. Do thou go there now, Jack, and ask for work. Take this penn'orth of pins." Jack put them in his pocket. "As soon as thou reachest the door, Jack, he will summon thee to table. Put the pins into the mug thou wilt see upon the table. Go there, Jack, and do as I have bidden thee." ℭ So off Jack went, and came to the old castle and knocked at the door. And the giant came out. He asked Jack what he wanted. "Any odd jobs." "Come in. Art thou hungry?" The giant brought him food. He ate. "Wilt thou have a drop of this, Jack?" Jack rose from his chair and smelt it. "Not I!" quoth Jack, "I will have a drop of ale." The giant went out of the room. Jack got up, and emptied the pins into the mug. ℭ Here comes the giant, and gives him a mug of ale. "Dost thou not like the other drink?" asks he. "Not I!" quoth Jack, "I would sooner have a drop of ale." ℭ Lo! now

the mug is in the giant's hand. He stirred it before he drank
it. After he had stirred it he tossed it off & sat down. He grew
ill. He grew worse and worse. He fell down and died. Jack
hurried off and left him there. ℂ Now Jack returns to the
little old man. He went up to him. "How didst thou get
on, Jack?" "I have killed him." "Now then, Jack, thou must
take the cows for the maids to milk." ℂ Here he is at the
hall with the cows, and every cow was there. Out comes the
old squire to count the cows. He went back and told his wife
that all the cows were there. Now the young lady goes out
to see for herself. She came back, and her mother would not
believe that not one cow was missing. ℂ Jack was sitting at
the table getting his supper. The young lady had a talk with
him. Quoth the young lady: "To-morrow, Jack, I am going to
be slain. I should like thee to be there to see." "I cannot come,
I am afraid of the master." Jack gave the plum to the lady. The
lady asked: "Where didst thou get this?" and ate it. Jack got up
and went outside to bed. ℂ He rose betimes in the morning to
take the cows for the maids to milk. He returned to the house
to get his breakfast. And there was the young lady preparing
some food for him to take down to the fields. Jack finished
his meal. Now he takes his victuals and goes out. The maids
had finished milking. ℂ Now Jack drives the cows down to
the fields. And there was the old dwarf waiting for him, and
Jack gave him the food. The little old man sat down and ate
his bellyful. "Up with thee to the castle, Jack! Thou knowest
that great gate? Here is a key for thee to open it. Enter: thou
wilt see a black steed and black raiment. Dress thee and take
the steed. Thou wilt see a sword there. Mount thy steed, and
let him go to the river and drink. Go thou and vanquish the
dragon: he is going to fight with the lady." ℂ Jack set out
and reached the place, and all the people were amazed at this
black horse and rider. Just as he drew near the lady, the dragon

began to vomit fire upon her. Jack smote him with his sword and felled him beneath the horse's feet. The horse struck at him with his hoofs, and Jack with his sword. The horse vomited the water he had drunk and extinguished the fire. Jack and his horse fought well; they nearly made an end of the dragon, and left him on the field. And Jack returned, and put the horse in his stall and changed his clothes. He replaced everything, locked the gate and went his way. ⫶ Now he goes down for the cows and takes them home to be milked. He brought them to the hall, and the old squire was standing outside to count the cows. They were every one there. ⫶ Jack went indoors to get his supper. The young lady was inside and talked to him. And the lady fell in love with Jack. Jack gave her another plum, and she began to eat. "How delicious this is! Where dost thou get them?" "Down yonder!" "Well, Jack, to-morrow I am going again to be slain by the dragon. Canst thou be there, Jack? I wish that thou couldst come to see me." "No, I cannot come. I should like to go, but I am afraid of the master." "I know that my father would let thee come if thou wert to ask." "I do not like to ask." Then the lady left the room and Jack went out. ⫶ He rose next morning at dawn to take the cows to be milked, and went into the house to get his breakfast. The lady had prepared his victuals; she asked whether there was enough. "Put in a little more, please." The lady gave him more. ⫶ Now Jack sets off down the fields with the cows. There was the little dwarf waiting for him. Jack gave him the food. "There thou art, Jack, take the key and go up to the castle. I will look after the cows. Open the great gate. Thou wilt see a white steed and white raiment. Take the clothes and dress thee and mount thy steed and take thy sword, and let thy steed go to the river & drink. Off with thee, and lash thy steed to a gallop!" ⫶ He reached the place and a great crowd was there. And the lady saw this knight approaching, and she was amazed. The dragon began to vomit fire upon the lady, but again the horse extinguished it with the water he had drunk. And Jack struck him with the sword, and the horse pounded him with his hoofs. He knocked him to smithereens, and the dragon lay prostrate: he could not stir. ⁋ Jack returned, and put the horse back where he had found him, and the clothes in their right place, and went down to fetch the cows. And the little old man was there. "Jack, rise at dawn to-morrow. To-morrow will be the last day; and tell the lady to give thee a trifle more food." ⁋ Now Jack goes off with the cows, and back to the hall; and out came the maids to milk. Jack went indoors, and the young lady was there, and she gave him his supper. Jack gave her a plum and the lady ate it. "How delicious, Jack!" Jack began his meal. And now the young lady is preparing his victuals for the morning. "I am going forth at break of day to be slain." The lady left the room and Jack went outside to bed. ⁋ He rose at dawn to fetch the cows. He drove them up, and went into the house for his breakfast. And the lady was in the room. "This is the last day, Jack, and I shall be slain; thou wilt see me no more." "I should like to be there, but I cannot come. I must look after the cows." Jack finished eating and went off with the cows. ⁋ He wandered down the fields, and there was the little dwarf. "Haste thee, Jack, and go up to the castle. There is the key. Thou knowest where the place is. Open the gate and walk in. Thou wilt see a red steed and red raiment. Dress thee and mount thy steed, and take thy sword & sally forth, and let thy steed go to the river." ⁋ The horse drank the river dry, and galloped off. And he reached the place and a huge crowd was waiting for this champion to appear. They saw him approaching, and all the people were amazed. The dragon vomited fire on the lady's hair & scorched it. Lo! Jack makes for him, and thrusts his sword through him. And the horse pounded him with his hoofs, while poor Jack smote him with his sword. And the horse felled him to the earth, and vomited all the water over him. And Jack struck off his head with his sword & slew him. The lady cut off a lock of Jack's hair with her golden scissors. ⦿ Jack returned, and put the horse back in his stall, and replaced the clothes & everything else, and locked the gate and went his way. Now Jack goes to fetch the cows, and he found the old dwarf there. Said the old man to Jack: "The lady is going to give a banquet. She wants to discover the knight, the one who slew the dragon. When thou comest down in the morning, Jack, bring me thy food." "Very well! I will bring plenty of food for thee when I come down in the morning." "Here thou art, Jack! give this plum to the lady." ⦿ Now Jack returns to the house with the cows; and the maids came out to milk. And Jack went indoors to get his supper, and the lady was inside. She told Jack about the knight. Jack was glad to hear it. He put his hand in his pocket and gave her a plum, and the lady ate it. Quoth the lady: "I will prepare thy victuals now. There will be no time to do it in the morning." "That will do very well," said Jack. Then Jack went out to bed. ⦿ He rose in the morning and went to fetch the cows. He brought the cows to the hall for the maids to milk. He went into the house to get his breakfast. The lady was there to give him his victuals. And the lady said to him: "This place will be packed with gentry to-day. I must hurry off, for I have much to do." ⦿ Then the lady hastened away and left Jack, and Jack finished his breakfast and went out. Now Jack goes down to the fields with the cows. And the little old dwarf was waiting for him. "How art thou this morning, Jack?" "I am quite well. Art thou well?" "Yes, but I want some food," quoth the old man. "There is plenty of food over there, go and take it." The little old man went and sat down by the food, and ate his bellyful. ⦿ "Now, Jack," quoth the old dwarf, "thou hast not any time to linger. Thou must go to the castle, and thou knowest where the red steed is kept. Leave the steed, and dress thee in the red suit, and put on thy old clothes over it, when the girl comes out to summon thee." ⁑ Now Jack sets off, and leaves the old dwarf. He went to the great gate, & opened it and entered, and donned the red suit, and then put on his old clothes over it. Then he went out to clean the stable. ⁑ There was a dais prepared for the lady in the banqueting-hall. And there was a high table, and food was upon the table. All the young gentlemen were present. Each one that entered walked up to the lady and laid his head on her lap. And a lock of Jack's hair was in her hand, that she might see whether that was the right man. "No, that is not the one!" Another gallant appeared, and walked up to the lady and laid his head on her lap. "That is not the man!" So did they all: it was none of them. ⁑ Then quoth the old squire: "Go and fetch the Butler." He walked across the chamber to the lady, and laid his head on her lap. She took up the lock of hair and looked at it. "No, that is not the man!" ⁑ Quoth the old squire: "Go and fetch the Coachman." He walked into the chamber and up to the lady, and laid his head on her lap. And the lock of hair was in her hand & she looked at it. "No, that is not the man!" ⁑ Quoth the squire: "Go and fetch the Boots." He came in, and walked across the chamber to the lady. He laid his head on her lap. "No, that is not the man!" He took himself off. ⁑ Quoth the old squire: "Go and fetch the Cowherd." Lo! he comes in, and people caught a glimpse of a red coat beneath his old rags, and recognized him. He walked across the chamber up to the lady, and laid his head on her lap. And the lock of hair was in the lady's hand. And the lady recognized him as soon as she saw him. "This is the man!" "What! that man?" exclaimed the old squire. ⁑ Now Jack went out to strip off his rags, and lo! he returns wearing his grand clothes and a sword. He enters the chamber. As soon as the squire beheld him thus arrayed, he stood up and gave him his hand. He was to be the lady's husband. ℂ Jack retired, and the young lady & the old squire discussed the date of the marriage. "When dost thou wish it to be?" asked the young lady of her father. "In a week," said the old squire; "but when wouldst thou like the wedding?" "The week after that." "Do ye two go to the city to be married. When the wedding is over, come home. There is enough here for both of you. Everything will be ready when ye return." Quoth the young lady to her father: "That will do." ℂ The couple went off, and were wedded, and returned home, and the place was packed with gentry, and there was dancing and fiddling. After it was all over, the old squire had a talk with his daughter. "Wouldst thou like to go and live where the giant used to live?" "Yes, I would, if that is thy will." ℂ And Jack and his lady went to live in that castle, and the lady's father sent two maidservants there and two menservants. ℂ A few years afterwards the old squire died, and also his wife. And Jack had a family. Jack's eldest son married, and Jack gave the castle to his eldest son. He is there to this day: I left him there. ℂ That is all.

THE KING OF THE HERRINGS.

SOMEWHERE VERY FAR AWAY lived a Quarry-man. He was old and his wife had never borne him any children. At last a son was born to them, and all the neighbours were amazed—the man and woman were so old to have a child. ⦅ The father died & the son took his place. And lo! an old man passes by, and the youth gazed upon him. Now the old man asks him: "Wilt thou come with me to seek our living?" "Yes," quoth Jack. "Then say that thou wishest me turned into an old nag." "Done!" quoth Jack. "Get on my back; let us be off." ⦅ So off they set, the old nag and Jack, along the road. Said the old nag to Jack: "If thou shouldst chance to see or hear anyone in trouble on the way, go and find out what is the matter, and if thou canst do aught, do it." ⦅ And lo and behold! here we are upon the road. And here we are taking the hill! And now the pair are well on their way. Quoth Jack to the nag: "I hear something." "Go and see what it is." Jack got down from the horse's back to see what was there. He saw a little herring that the tide had left stranded. Jack picked it up and put it back in the water. And lo! the fish swam right up to him. Quoth the fish to Jack: "Whatsoever I can do for thee, call upon me, the King of the Herrings, & I will do it." ⦅ Away they go over the hill. "Jack, touch nothing that thou seest, even though it be the finest thing thine eyes have ever beheld." And lo! the wind blew a feather into his mouth. Twice or thrice did he spit it out. Back came the feather again. He thought it a pretty feather, and put it in his pocket. ⦅ And now they come to an old castle. And they hear a great uproar within the castle. "Go and see what is the matter," said the old nag. Jack went up to the castle and knocked at the gate. No one came out to him. He opened the gate and went in to see what was happening. He saw a giant lying on a bed, helpless.

He could do nothing for himself: he was ill. There was no maid-servant to give him food. "What ails thee, friend?" "I have no serving-wench in this place. Go, bring me food and a tankard of ale from below." The giant ate his bellyful, and bade Jack call upon him if ever he could do aught for him. ℂ Now the pair are going downhill! Quoth the old nag: "What didst thou see on the mountain?" "I saw nothing but a little feather which the wind blew into my mouth." "Didst thou take the feather?" "Yes, I have it in my pocket." "This feather will bring us misfortune; but keep it, do not let it go." ℂ And now the young man went to a grand mansion to look for work. The master of the house came out to see his craft with the quill. It was excellent: thou couldst not beat it. ℂ Then he went in search of some place to sleep in. The master invited him to sleep in the house. "Nay," said Jack, "I will go out to my old nag in the stable." ℂ Everyone marvelled at his feats with this feather. One day the man-servant said to his master: "Call him hither, master, that I may get hold of his quill." The master called him. He came. The servant took away the quill, and put another on the table in its place. "Master, I have it! the man who brought the feather here can bring the bird too." ℂ Said Jack to the old nag: "The master wants the bird." "Go, Jack, and ask him to give thee three days and three purses of gold." They set off in search of the bird. "Jack, go up to the castle and walk in. Thou wilt see a company feasting at table. Touch nothing. In a corner thou wilt see a draggle-tailed bird in a cage. Go, take it, but tarry not." ℂ Out he comes to the old nag carrying the bird. The pair returned bringing the bird with them. Now the master & his servant talked it over as they looked at the bird. The servant said to the master: "The bird is pretty; the lady is prettier still." Quoth the servant: "The man who brought the bird here can bring the lady too." ℂ Jack went out to the old nag and told him that the master wanted the lady. "I warned thee about the feather, Jack. Go and ask him for three days and three purses of gold." Jack went back to ask the master. He got the money & the three days. ⓒ And away they go! They talk together on the road. Said the old nag to Jack: "Jack, do thou wish me turned into a ship upon the sea." As soon as the word was spoken, there was the ship on the sea. ⓒ And here they are going aboard! (The ship was laden with silk.) Now they are sailing beneath the castle. "Jack, go up to the castle and ask to see the lady. She whom thou wilt see coming forth to thee is not the lady; ask to see the lady herself." ⓒ Jack went to the castle. He knocked at the gate, and lo! a lady appears. She was not the mistress; she was the housekeeper. Said Jack to her: "I want to see the lady herself." The servant went in to tell her mistress. Anon the lady comes out. Jack told her that there was a ship at anchor below the castle: and she stepped down to look at the silk. The lady came aboard, & one of the crew led her to the cabin where the silk was stored. Jack remained on deck. He weighed anchor and the ship sailed away. ⓒ And now they are far out at sea. By this time the lady had finished her business and come on deck. When she saw that she had been trapped, she felt in her pocket, pulled out her keys and flung them into the sea. The sea turned red as blood, and was troubled by a mighty storm. ⓒ Here they are back at the mansion! And Jack leads the lady inside. The master & the servant spoke a few words together. Quoth the servant to his master: "The man who brought the lady here can bring the castle too." ⓒ Jack went out to the old nag & told him. "Well, Jack, I warned thee about the feather, that it would bring us misfortune. Go back, Jack, and ask him for three days and three sacks of gold." Jack went back and got them. ⓒ When they were both well on their way, the old nag asked Jack: "What did the giant say to thee?" "He promised he would do anything for me." "Go to him and tell him what thou wantest." ⓒ So up Jack goes to the castle. He told the giant what he wanted, and the giant fell a-laughing at him. He sent him out to fetch his chain, but Jack could not lift a single link. Again the giant burst out laughing, and straightway strode out, picked up the chain, and slung it over his shoulder. ℂ Now they both hasten down to the lady's castle. The giant fastened the chain to the castle, put it on his back and carried it down to the lady's biding-place. There was a high wall round the lady's home and the gate was locked. Quoth the lady to Jack: "I want my keys: I cannot open the gate." ℂ Again Jack went out to consult the old nag. "Jack, I warned thee about the feather. Go back and ask for such and such things." He went back and got what he wanted. ℂ So here they are again journeying along the road! "Jack, what did the little herring say to thee?" "Whatsoever I can do for thee, I will do: shouldst thou have need of me, thou must call upon the King of the Herrings." ℂ Jack and the old nag made for the spot where he had found the fish, and hailed him. Lo! the fish swam up to him. Jack told him about the keys. "I will go in search of them, Jack." He disappeared and was gone a great while. He came back; but he had not found the keys. "I have not found them, Jack, I will try again." And again he was gone a great while. At last he reappeared, and he had found the keys and he gave them to Jack. The herring swam away and the old nag and Jack returned home. ℂ Jack handed the keys to the lady. The lady asked Jack: "Which wouldst thou rather, Jack, that thy head or that thy master's head be cut off?" Jack stopped to think what answer he should make. Then he said to the lady: "Do not slay him, slay me." Quoth the lady: "Thou hast answered well, Jack, thou hast answered well. Hadst thou not spoken thus thou wouldst have been slain. Now it is thy master who will be slain." ℂ Jack and the lady were married and the master was slain. And the lady and Jack still live in the castle. ℂ And now thou hast my tale.

THE DEVIL'S TALE.

THERE WAS A LITTLE COTTAGE where an old woman lived with her son. Her son was a great big man. And a field away stood a fine hall. And the old woman used to go to this hall every hour to get a loaf of barley bread, and a great potful of buttermilk. And thus it was for three years. ⁋ And one morning the squire asked the old woman: "Whom hast thou to support that thou needest so much food?" "I have no one to keep except myself and my son." "I will give thee nothing more; send thy son hither, I wish to see him." ⁋ The old woman returned to her cottage. Quoth she to her son: "He will give me nothing more; go up to the hall, he wishes to see thee." "What does he want with me?" said the son. And up he went to the hall. ⁋ And here is the squire out on the doorstep! And he looks the man up and down. "Canst thou work?" quoth he. "What IS work?" asked this big man. "Come here and I will show thee"; and he led him into the shippon. The farmer took a pitchfork in his hand. "This is the way," quoth he, and tosses some cowdung through the door. "This is the way I want thee to do it." ⁋ "That is naught!" quoth the giant, and he seized the fork, and threw all the dung out in one throw. The farmer was amazed to see him. ⁋ "I have a herd of cows on the other side of the river; go and drive them all up to the house. Lead them through the water without wetting the hoofs of a single one." ⁋ The giant took a sack and a carving-knife, crossed the river, and ran after the cows, and caught one. He chopped off her four hoofs and put them in the sack. Thus he dealt with the whole herd. Now they are hoofless, every one! ⁋ He drove them through the water and up to the house. There was the squire at the door. The giant threw the sack down at his feet: all the hoofs tumbled out of it. "Look," quoth he, "are they wet?" ⁋ When the squire saw what the man had done, there was a mighty quarrel; but the two were reconciled after a time. ⁅ "Now," said the farmer, "I want thee to do another job for me. Yonder in the forest I have a cart and three horses. Thou wilt find some men there loading the cart with timber, and thou hast naught to do except to say to the horses: 'Now then, gee up!'" ⁅ The man went off. He called to the horses: "Gee up!" Not one of them would budge. He unharnessed the leader, fastened his four feet together, and flung him into the cart. "Now then, gee up!" he called to the other two. Neither of them would budge. He unharnessed them both, bound their four feet, and flung them into the cart. Then he went between the shafts himself, and dragged everything—cart, timber, and the three horses—up to the hall. ⁅ Out came the old squire: he was amazed to see this feat. The giant left the cart before the door, and went to get his dinner of butter-milk and barley-bread. The old squire asked him: "Whence didst thou get thy strength?" No, he would not tell. ⁅ Said the squire to him: "Down yonder in the field is a great lake. I want thee to drain it for me." ⁅ The giant went off; he felled a huge tree. He reached the lake; he thrust the tree into the bank beneath the lake, and let all the water escape. ⁅ Early in the morning the old squire went down to the lake to look at it. The water was all dried up. He asked the man again: "Whence didst thou get thy strength?" He would not tell. ⁅ "I will show thee what strength really is," said the giant. He seized a great iron chain. He fastened the chain round the hall with all the people in it, and dragged it down, and set it beside his own wretched little hut. ⁅ Quoth the squire to him in the morning: "If thou wilt tell me where thou didst get thy strength, I will give thee all my sheep, and all my cows, and all my horses." ⁅ The giant said naught. He put his hand in his pocket, and drew out a little white button. "Here, take this," quoth he. ⁅ Now the squire was a man who would believe anything. He put the button in his pocket, gave all he possessed to the giant & went away to a distant place. ℂ Three days passed. The squire saw that nothing was going to come of it. Quoth he to himself: "That man has cheated me: the devil must be on his side. I will make my way back to him at once." ℂ He went back and knocked softly at the door. Out came the giant. The squire greeted him with the words: "Thou art the devil!" "Aye," answered the giant, "the devil himself!" And he knocked the squire flat. And there the devil still lives. ℂ And I deserve a big pudding for telling thee this lie.

THERE WAS A MILL, A YOUNG MAN, and his maidservant. Now this man was a great gambler. No one could beat him: he beat everybody. ⁋ There came a gentleman to him, and he walked straight into the miller's room. The two had a word together. "Wilt thou play?" asked the gentleman of the young man: the cards were on the table. "Yes," quoth the young man. ⁋ Now the two are at their game. The miller beat the gentleman. The gentleman asked Jack: "What wouldst thou have?" "I would have a castle yonder." As soon as he said the word, there was the castle. ⁋ The gentleman said to Jack: "Wilt have another game?" "Yes," quoth Jack. And now the two are at their game, and the gentleman beat him. And the gentleman said: "This time thou must find my castle. My name is *The Green Man Who Lives in No Man's Land*. And if thou dost not find my castle in a year and a day, I will cut off thy head." ℂ Time passed. And here is Jack setting off on horseback to seek for this man. He travelled a long, long way, and there was frost and deep snow. Night came upon him. He was hungry. He saw a little house near the road, and he got off his horse & went to the door. He knocked at the door. ℂ Lo! a little old woman comes out to him. Jack asked for a bed. "All right!" quoth the old woman, "come in." He sat down by the fire. The old woman and Jack had a talk together. The old woman got supper for Jack. Jack asked the old woman whether she knew a man whose name was *The Green Man Who Lives in No Man's Land*. "No," quoth the old woman, "never have I heard the name. I will let thee know in the morning, if a quarter of the whole world knows." ℂ In the morning they had breakfast. The old woman went outside and called Jack to her. A ladder was standing by the door. The old woman climbed up on to the roof and blew a horn. ℂ Lo! the folk come hurrying up. She asked them whether they knew or had heard—the old woman spoke the name to them—whether they knew of this man. "His name is *The Green Man Who Lives in No Man's Land*." "No," quoth the folk, they had never heard the name. The folk departed. ℂ The old woman blew again. Lo! the birds come flying to her now. She asked the birds whether they knew or had heard of such a man—*The Green Man Who Lives in No Man's Land*. They had never heard the name. "Then begone!" They flew away. ℂ The old woman had a talk with Jack. "Farther on I have a sister. Go there; she will speak more wisely to thee, she knows more than I know. Take my horse, and leave thine here." She gave him a ball of thread, and told him to throw the ball over the horse's ears. Jack did so, and set off. ℂ He came to the house, just as the old woman had told him. The second old woman called Jack into the house. "It is a long time," quoth she, "since I have seen my sister's horse." ℂ He put the horse in the stable. The old woman called Jack into the house to have supper. The two sat down to table and ate: they finished eating. The two had a talk together. Jack asked the old woman whether she knew or had heard the name. Jack spoke the name to her—*The Green Man Who Lives in No Man's Land.* "No," quoth the old woman, "never have I heard such a name. I will let thee know in the morning if half the world knows." They went to their beds. ℂ In the morning they dressed themselves. The two came down and ate their breakfast. They finished. Then the old woman went outside. She called Jack to her. The old woman climbed up the ladder and blew a horn. ℂ Lo! half the world comes hurrying up to her. She asked them whether they knew or had heard of the man. The old woman spoke his name—*The Green Man Who Lives in No Man's Land.* No, they had never heard the name. "Begone!" ℂ The old woman blew the horn again. Lo! half the birds in the world come flying to the old woman. She asked them whether they knew or had heard of such a man. "His name is *The Green Man Who Lives in No Man's Land.*" No, they had never heard the name. "Then begone!" ℂ "Come in, Jack. I have a sister, and if she know not, then there is none who knows. Take my horse, Jack, and leave my sister's horse here. Take a ball of thread and throw it over the horse's ears." He did so. ℂ Now he comes to the house. And here is the eldest sister at the door. She stared at Jack as he rode up. "That is my sister's horse: I have not seen him for a great while. Put the horse in the stable, and give him some food." And Jack did so. ℂ The old woman called Jack into the house to have supper. The two sat down to table. They ate and finished eating. Jack talked with the old woman, and asked whether she knew the name of such a man. "No," quoth the old woman, "I have never heard it. I will let thee know in the morning." Then they went to their beds. ❡ In the morning the old woman got up, made a fire, put the kettle on the fire, and called Jack to come downstairs. He did so. He came to the table to have his breakfast. They finished. Now Jack and the old woman both sit by the fire, and Jack smokes his pipe. And Jack has a talk with the old woman. The old woman got up and went outside. She called Jack to her. The old woman climbed up the ladder and blew a horn. ❡ Lo! all the people in the world come hurrying up to her. She asked them whether they knew about this man. The old woman spoke the name to them—*The Green Man Who Lives in No Man's Land*. No, they had never heard the name. "Begone!" quoth the old woman. The folk departed. "Wait a little, Jack! I will call all the birds that are in the world." The old woman blew the horn again. Lo! all the birds come flying to her. She asked them whether they knew where such a man was. "I will tell you his name—*The Green Man Who Lives in No Man's Land*." All the birds said "No," they had never heard the name. ❡ The old woman came down and opened her book to see whether all the birds were there. She found from her book that there was one bird missing. ❡ The old woman went back to the roof of the house and blew the horn again. Lo! the bird appears. It was the eagle. She said to him: "Wretch! where hast thou been all this long while?" "I was with a certain man. I have come from the country of *The Green Man Who Lives in No Man's Land*." He told her where it was. "Begone! That is all I want to know." ❡ "Come in, Jack, that I may tell thee. Leave my sister's horse here, and take my horse; and take a ball of thread & throw it over the horse's ears." ❡ Jack mounted his horse. And the old woman said to Jack: "Touch nothing! let the horse go. Thou wilt see a great lake, Jack, and on the lake three white birds; dismount and hide thee by the lake. Thou wilt see these three white birds come nigh thee, and shake down their feathers and go to bathe. Two will go into the lake to bathe, and the third will stay & shake down her feathers. The three will bathe. Arise then, Jack; go, take the feathers and keep them. The third will come to thee and want her feathers. Do not give them up. Tell her to carry thee over the lake to her father's castle."   ℂ Jack set off, and he found the lake just where the old woman had said. When the last swan went into the lake, Jack stole her feathers.   ℂ "Carry me over the lake to thy father's castle!" "No," quoth she, "I have no father." "Yes," quoth Jack. "No," quoth she again.   ℂ Lo! she weeps; she wants her feathers back from him. "Carry me over the lake and thou shalt have thy feathers." "Get on my back. But do not tell my father, when thou goest up to the castle, that I carried thee over the lake." She carried him over, and when she had carried him over, the swan turned into a young lady.   ℂ Now Jack goes up to the castle. He went to the door and knocked. Lo! the lord comes out. "Hast found the house, Jack? Then one of my daughters has been with thee." "Say not so, I have not seen one of them." "Come in." He gave him food. The lord told him to clean out the stable. "If thou dost not perform this task, thy head shall be cut off."   ℂ Jack pulled off his coat to do the work. For one spadeful that he threw out, three came in. He grew tired. He threw the spade down. He flung the thing away and seated himself. He was weary.   ℂ Presently the lady came to him, the youngest lady. She brought food. "Get up, Jack, and eat." Jack got up and ate. While he was eating, the stable was cleansed: all the filth was carried out. "Jack, do not tell my father that I was here with thee."   ℂ Now the old lord comes out and goes into the stable. "I know, Jack, that my daughter has been with thee." "I have not seen thy daughter. I know naught: naught do I know of thy daughters." The lord went away. ⚌ Out came Jack. Presently the lord appears again, and he calls Jack. "I have trees that I want thee to fell before midday." Now the two go outside, that he may point out the trees to Jack: and great trees they were. "There they are, Jack! dost see them?" "Yes," quoth Jack. ⚌ Jack pulls off his coat. He felled three trees. "If I were at home I would die there: but as things are, it is here I must die." He sat down and began to weep. The young lady came to him with his dinner. "Get up, Jack, & have thy dinner." Jack ate: he made an end of eating. ⚌ "Stand up, Jack." He stood up and he saw the trees were all felled. "Jack, do not tell my father that I was with thee. My father will ask thee whether I was with thee. But thou must say 'No'." The lady went away. ⚌ Now the old lord comes out. "Yes, Jack, I know that one of my daughters has been with thee." "Do not lie: I know naught about thy daughters, none of them." The two come back to the castle. "I want a barn built up yonder," quoth the lord. And Jack has to build this barn, and he has to take one feather from every bird to make the thatch. ⚌ He built the place, but the whole thatch was lacking. He caught one little red bird; he took a single feather from it, and let the little red bird go. He looked at the place. He sat down, and knew not what to do. ⚌ And there he was sitting when the young lady came with his tea. "Get up, Jack, and have thy tea." Jack got up to eat it. He finished. "Thy task is done. Tell my father, Jack, that thou carest naught for him nor his daughters." ⚌ Said the lady to Jack: "There is a mountain in the lake, about a mile out, and a bird will come there & will lay one egg. To-morrow my father will tell thee about it, Jack. And thou must thyself offer to go and get it. Do thou go to the lake, and I will be there." ⚌ The morrow came. The old lord told Jack what he had to do. "Pooh!" quoth Jack, "that is naught." And now here is Jack by the lake. He sat down. Presently the lady came with his breakfast. "Have thy breakfast, Jack." He finished eating. "Pull off thy shoe, Jack. Wish that thy shoe be turned into a boat." So it was. ℂ Lo! the twain enter the boat. And they come to the mountain. He could not climb it. "Wish my fingers to be turned into a ladder for thee to climb up by." As soon as Jack said the word, there was the ladder. And the lady said to him: "When thou goest up the steps, pick up each rung one after another. Do not forget a single one." He missed one, and broke one of the lady's fingers. They got the egg. ℂ Now the pair are returning. "Say to my father, Jack, when thou goest back to the castle, and my father asks thee whether I have been with thee, say thou: 'No, I know naught about thee nor about thy daughters'." ℂ The old lord said: "One of my daughters has been with thee." "No," quoth Jack, "I have not seen them." "I have a little job for thee in the morning." "I care not what it is." ℂ Jack was out betimes, and the young lady found him & had a talk with him. "Jack, I have two sisters, and to-morrow my father will turn us into three swans. We three sisters will fly over the house thrice. And my father will be with thee & will tell thee to choose the same one thrice. When we fly over the house, Jack, do thou choose the first one, and when we come back choose the middlemost, and when we come back again choose the last one." ℂ Morning came. The old lord and the old lady and Jack were out together before the door. Lo! the three white birds fly over the house. "I will have the first one." Lo! they are returning. "I will have the middlemost." Lo! they are flying back again. "Which is it now?" Said Jack to the lord: "I will have the last one." "Yes, Jack, thou hast won her: she shall be thy wife." ℂ Now they are married. The old lord died, and the old lady as well; and now Jack is in the castle. ℂ And that is all.

THE THREE SISTERS.

THERE WAS A COTTAGE and there lived in this cottage an old man and his wife. They had three children, and these three children were three little sisters. And they dwelt there summer after summer until their father and mother died. ℂ And two summers after their father and mother died, there came to the cottage a little old woman who wore a red cloak. And she went to the door and begged for a cup of tea. "No," said the eldest sister, "we have not enough for ourselves." "I will bind thy head and thine eyes, if I bind not thy whole body," said the crone to her. With that she departed. ℂ And now these three sisters grew poor. And one day the eldest sister said to the two others: "I am going to seek work somewhere. And do ye two stay here to look after the house. But if ye see the spring dried up & blood in the ladle, some evil has befallen me. Come then, one of you, in search of me." And so in the morning when they arose they used to look for the tokens of which their elder sister had spoken. ℂ Let us leave the two younger sisters for a time and follow the eldest one. ℂ The eldest sister journeyed to where the devil never wound his horn and the cock never crew. Night fell. Presently she saw a little man in a red jerkin. This little red-jerkined fellow was brother to the old woman of the red cloak. And before the girl asked aught of him, he put a question to her. "Art thou seeking work?" "Yes," replied the girl. ℂ Little Red Jerkin gave her no hint of the trial that lay before her. He opened a gate: "Go up there, and thou wilt get work!" ℂ And up she climbed. There were little white stones all the way up the hill. "Stop and look!" cried one white stone. The girl stopped and looked at the stone. She was bewitched into a trance and transformed into a white pebble. Thus did old Red Cloak bind her head and her eyes with a spell. And now she has bound her whole body. ℂ Let us leave her there and return to the two younger sisters. ℂ One morning the second sister arose and ran to the door to look. She opened the door, and there was the spring dried up & blood in the ladle. Horror overwhelmed her when she beheld these things. "Some evil has befallen my sister," she cried to the youngest girl. Then the spring flowed and the ladle was bright again. Now she, in her turn, said to her younger sister: "If thou seest the spring dried up and blood in the spoon, some misfortune has overtaken me. Come then and seek for me." ℂ Let us leave the youngest girl now and follow her who set out in search of the eldest sister. ℂ She journeyed to where the devil never wound his horn and the cock never crew, until she met this same man in the red jerkin. And before she could utter a word to him, Red Jerkin spoke to her. "Art thou looking for work?" asked he. "No," answered the girl, "I am looking for my sister." "Thy sister is up yonder; she has found work, and is doing well." ℂ The gate was opened and the girl climbed up the hill. "Stop!" cried one white stone. The girl did not pause, but went straight on. "Look!" called another stone to her. The girl went on. "Lo! here is thy sister," cried a third stone. She stood still & looked round when she heard this news about her sister. And she was bewitched into a magic trance and transformed into a white pebble. ℂ Let us return now to the youngest sister who was at home. ℂ She arose one morning and went to the door and opened it. There was no water in the spring: it was dried up. There was blood in the ladle! Then the youngest sister burst into tears. ℂ But she had more spirit than the other two. She knew not where they had gone: she knew not where to seek them. So, after making fast the door, she took the road on which she had seen her sisters set out. ℂ And she journeyed to where the devil never wound his horn & the cock never crew, until she met the little fellow in the red jerkin. Before he could open his mouth, the youngest sister spoke to him. She got in the first word. She asked him about work. "Yes, there is work for thee." His heart was well-nigh broken, because the maiden had got in the first word. ❧ He opened the gate and the girl climbed up the hill. As she climbed, one white stone cried to her "Stop!" The girl went on. "Look!" cried a second stone. "This is the place!" cried a third stone. The maiden was quite fearless. She paid no heed to them. "Lo! here are thy two sisters," cried yet another stone. "Kiss them, then," quoth she. And on she sped until there were no more stones & she reached the little old woman in the red cloak. ❧ When Red Cloak espied the girl she fell on her knees before her. "Hast thou found me then, little lady?" "I have," quoth the little lady. ❧ And now, lo & behold! all that slumbrous spell was broken. And all these white stones were restored to their former shapes. It was this maiden who had broken the whole enchantment. My dear God had put it into her heart to achieve all this and to have no fear. ❧ And she went to her two sisters & led them up to the old woman in the red cloak. "Here are my two sisters," quoth she. "I know them," answered Red Cloak. "But it is thou who art mistress here now. All is left in thy hands. Do as thou wilt." "I thank thee, good aunt." ❧ Red Cloak showed the youngest sister where all the treasure was. Then the girl gave her two sisters each a bagful of gold, and charged them to send her word if any mischance should ever again befall them. And they both fell on their knees before their youngest sister. They were escorted home. ❧ And she became the greatest lady in all that land, far and wide, and she married Red Jerkin. And they live there happily to this day.

THE LITTLE CROP-TAILED HEN.

ONCE UPON A TIME there were two great big mansions. In one lived a widow and in the other a widower. The old lady had a daughter and so had the old gentleman. The old lady's daughter was an ill-favoured little creature and a hunchback to boot. As for the old gentleman's daughter, she was a beautiful lady. The widower and the widow married. Then they all lived together in the old gentleman's hall. ℂ The little hunchback had to go down to the well with a pail to fetch water. She took the pail and went down. There was a cottage near the gate, & a little old woman dwelt there. The old woman was standing at the door, and she invited the hunchbacked girl to come in to have something to eat. The little hunchback grew angry. "Art thou not ashamed to ask me to enter such a wretched little hovel?" She left the old woman & went down to the well. ℂ She dipped her pail in the well. Three boars' heads arose. Quoth one: "Lift me, and wipe me, and comb me, and set me down softly." She struck them down with the pail. She dipped her pail in the well, and she drew it up again full of muddy water. She went home. "Why hast thou brought muddy water?" asked her mother. "I saw nothing but muddy water in the well." ℂ Now the other girl goes with the pail to the well. She went down the road, and she came to this old woman's cottage. The old woman was standing at the door. "Wilt thou come in, my lady, and have a mouthful to eat?" "Yes, that I will"; and in she went. She had something to eat. The old woman gave her a little sweet milk and some bread and butter. Now this old woman was a witch. ℂ The girl left the old woman and came out. She went down to the well. She dipped her pail in the well. Up sprang three boars' heads. Quoth one to the fair lady: "Lift me, & wipe me, and comb me, and set me down softly." She lifted him, she wiped him, she combed him, and she set him down softly. She filled her pail with water. The water was clear. She went home with it. ⟨. The old woman was bewildered. She knew not what to make of it. "How is it that *thou* canst fetch clear water, whilst thou, daughter, bringest muddy water?" ⟨. On the morrow it was the hunchback's turn to fetch water. She set off. She saw the old woman by the door. "Wilt thou come in, my lady, and have a mouthful to eat?" "Not I! art thou not ashamed to ask me?" She went to the well and dipped in her pail. Up sprang the three boars' heads. Quoth the second one: "Lift me, and wipe me, and comb me, and set me down softly." She struck them with the pail. She drew a pailful of muddy water and went home. Her mother was furious to see such muddy water again. ⟨. Now here is the other girl going to fetch water. Down she went, and she came to the little old woman's cottage. "Wilt thou come in, my lady, and have something to eat?" "Yes, that I will." She went in and had something to eat. She bade the old woman "Good day," and went down to the well. She dipped her pail in the water. Up sprang the three boars' heads. Quoth one: "Lift me, and wipe me, and comb me, and set me down softly." The fair girl did so, filled her pail with clear water, and went home. ⟨. The old woman was furious to see the beautiful girl bringing clear water. "How comes it that yon girl brings clear water whilst my child brings muddy water? I will send them both again to-morrow one after the other." ⟨. The morrow came. Down went the little hunchback. She saw the old witch. "Wilt thou come in, my lady, and have something to eat?" "Art thou not ashamed, thou old hag, to ask me to come in?" She went to the well and dipped in her pail. Up sprang the three boars' heads. "Lift me, and wipe me, & comb me, and set me down softly." She struck down the heads with her pail. ⟨. She turned to go home & saw three fine gentlemen standing before her. Said the eldest brother: "Here is a grand lady!" "Yes, brother," quoth the second. "What dost thou wish for this lady?" "I wish that one side of her hair shall be all lice." He asked the youngest brother: "And what dost thou wish for this lady?" "I wish that the other side shall be covered with nits." Now the eldest brother speaks: "She is hideous enough now; I wish that she be ten times more hideous when she reaches home." ℂ And now the fair girl goes to fetch water. She came to the little old woman's cottage. "Wilt thou come in, my lady, and have a mouthful to eat?" "Yes, that I will"; and in she went. She ate and came out. And she reached the well. She dipped in the pail. Up sprang the three boars' heads. "Lift me, & wipe me, and comb me, and set me down softly." She did so. The heads sank down. She drew a pailful of clear water. She turned her head: she saw three young gentlemen. The eldest brother said to the others: "Here is a lovely lady!" "Aye, she is a lovely lady indeed." "What dost thou wish for this young lady?" Quoth one: "I wish that one side of her hair shall be all gold." "What dost thou wish, brother?" "I wish that the other side shall be all silver." "And what is thy wish, brother?" they said to the eldest. "She is beautiful enough now; I wish that she be ten times more beautiful when she reaches home." ℂ And now the two half-sisters are at home. The old lady was aghast when she saw them—the one so hideous, and the other so wondrous fair. It made her ill to look upon them. She took to her bed and called her husband. "What shall we do with these two?" The old man pondered awhile and waited for his wife to speak before he said a word. "I know not what to do." Quoth the old lady: "Make a great chest and put them both into it, and cast them into the sea, and let them go whithersoever the wind carries them." It was done even as the old lady said. ℂ Lo! the two half-sisters are out at sea now. There they have been for a month. The fair lady found that she was pregnant. Her time came: she gave

birth to a Little Crop-tailed Hen. As soon as the little Hen
was born she looked upon her mother, and she looked upon
her ill-favoured aunt. "Mammy, who is this ugly creature
with thee?" ⁋ A week went by. The fair lady found a small
penknife in her pocket. She opened it. She examined the chest,
and cut a little hole in it with her knife. She thrust her finger
through the opening. She sawed away again to make the hole
larger. Then she put her head through to see where they were.
She saw fields. She went down below and said to the other
girl: "I have seen fields." The water grew shallower & shallower.
The wind blew them close up to the land. There they stopped
for a few days until she had made the hole wide enough for
them to creep through. ⁋ They escaped, left the chest behind,
and walked up an old by-lane. They found an empty barn. The
Little Hen went in to see what sort of a place it was. Out she
came and told her mother: "It is all right, there is plenty of
straw and the place is dry; come in!" ⁋ The three entered.
Quoth the Little Hen to her aunt: "Go and hide thyself in the
straw." She did so. The Little Hen heaped straw over her.
"And do thou, my Mammy, sit there; I am going to beg food
for thee." ⁋ The Little Hen went up the lane. She found a
great hall. She went up to the hall, and knocked at the door.
The butler came out to see who was there. He saw a Little
Crop-tailed Hen. He took no heed of her; he went in and shut
the door. ⁋ The Little Hen knocked at the door again. Out
came the butler. Quoth the Little Hen: "I want food for my
mammy." The butler went back to his master and mistress. "A
Little Crop-tailed Hen is out there, a-begging for her mother."
The master and mistress rose and came to the door. There was
the Little Hen. "I want food for my mammy." So in they
went, collected some victuals, brought them out and fastened
them upon the little Hen's back. ⁋ See! here is the Little Hen
setting off, and now she has reached the barn. "I have brought

food for thee, Mammy; give my ugly aunt something to eat, and then let her hide herself." ℂ That food lasted the three for three days. Now it was finished. The Little Hen goes again to the great hall. She got victuals in the same way as she got them before, and brought them home to her mother. ℂ Once more the food came to an end, and her mother told the Little Hen about it. "I will find food, Mammy." She went to the great hall. The butler knew what she wanted this time. And the old master and mistress agreed that they would watch where she went. ℂ Away went the Little Hen with the victuals. "I have brought food, Mammy; give my ugly aunt something to eat, and then let her hide herself." ℂ Now this time the old master and mistress followed the little Hen to watch where she went. They saw her go into the empty barn. They stopped the carriage. They sent the butler to peep through the window. He saw a beautiful lady with the Little Hen beside her, & they were eating. He told his master. His master alighted and went into the barn & spoke with her. He saw nothing of the hunchback; she was hidden in the straw. They took the lady and the Little Hen into their carriage & drove back to the great hall. ℂ The young master was there. As soon as the beauteous lady entered the great hall he gazed upon her; he loved her; he married her. The ugly lady was seized and sent home. The Little Hen stayed with her mother: no money could buy her. ℂ I was there, and I played the fiddle for them, & they paid me handsomely. That is all I have to tell.

THE LEAVES THAT HUNG BUT NEVER GREW

THERE WAS A LONELY LITTLE COTTAGE and a mother and her daughter living there. They were poor as poor could be, and the girl was forced to go and look for work. ℭ She set off and soon came to a great mansion. The lord asked her what she wanted; he called her in. "I am seeking work." "I will give thee work." And the task which he set her was to find the *Leaves that hung but never grew*. ℭ Away she went to seek them. As she was going down the lane she met a little dwarf. "Good day to thee," quoth he. He turned and looked after her. He went home and told his wife that he had seen a lovely young woman upon the road, but she was looking troubled. ℭ She journeyed on until she found a small house. Never before had she seen it: she was amazed. "This is all strange to me," she said to herself. ℭ She knocked at the door and out came an old witch. The young girl asked for work, and the witch bade her come into her little parlour. She saw a great black boar chained up in one corner. The old witch made some good tea for her, and gave her plenty to eat. She ate her bellyful, and made an end of eating. ℭ Now the only work which the old witch had to give her was to look after this black boar. The girl tended the boar for weeks. She knew not how to question the old witch concerning the leaves. ⓒ At last she grew weary and discontented. One day she exclaimed to the black boar: "O boar, boar, see the state my hands are in now! They were white and clean when I came here; but how rough and dirty are they now through looking after thee." "Wait a bit," quoth he, "and perhaps thou too wilt presently find thyself a black sow in the other corner. Tell me, why hast thou come hither?" "I came here to seek the *Leaves that hung but never grew.*" ⓒ No sooner were the words spoken than the boar was transformed into a young gentleman. "Go upstairs into the witch's bed-chamber," quoth he, "and put thy hand beneath her pillow. Thou wilt find a little wallet there. When thou layest thy hand upon the leaves, wish that the witch may remain asleep and not awaken." ⓒ She went upstairs; she laid her hand upon the wallet, and willed the witch to remain asleep and not awaken. She took the wallet, came downstairs, & gave half the leaves to the young gentleman. ⓒ "And now," quoth he, "let us devise three enchantments for the witch when she wakes and asks whether thou art coming to bed. First the poker shall say: 'I am raking out the fire'. Then the broom shall say: 'I am sweeping the house'. Lastly the chair shall say: 'I am coming now'." The girl wished these three things, and the two escaped together. ⓒ Lo! the witch awakens. She called the girl to come to bed. The poker answered: "I am raking out the fire." She called her again. The broom answered: "I am sweeping the house." She called her once more. The chair answered: "I am coming now." The girl came not. The witch called yet again: there was no answer. The witch was furious. She realized that the two had escaped. She summoned her daughter & told her to follow them, and whatsoever she should see on the road to bring home with her. ⓒ Lo! the two are speeding on their way. They saw the witch's daughter coming after them like the wind. Now she has almost overtaken them! Said the gentleman to the maiden: "Wish thyself a duck and me a running stream, and when she tries to catch thee dive beneath the water." She did so. The youth was transformed into a running stream and the girl turned herself into a duck. ⁋ And now the witch's daughter overtakes them! She comes up to the duck, and tries to catch her. "Duck, duck, pretty little duck," quoth she, "hast thou seen any one pass this way?" But every time that she came close to the little duck, the little duck dived beneath the water. ⁋ The witch's daughter went home and told her mother that she had seen a little duck swimming on the water, & naught besides. "Those were they!" cried the old witch. "Do thou return and fetch me but one feather from the duck, and I will very soon have them back again." She returned to get the feather. She saw neither duck nor stream. Both had vanished. She was broken-hearted. She went home and told the old witch that she could find nothing. ⁋ Lo! the two haste away until they reach a cross-road. Here they were obliged to part from one another. They made a pact that he should go to his home and return again to her. Quoth the girl to the youth: "When thou arrivest home, let not any of thy kinsfolk kiss thee, or thou wilt forget me." ⁋ This young man went home. His family had not seen him for years. His brothers and sisters hugged & kissed him, and he forgot all about the young maiden. ⁋ The girl waited a long time at the cross-roads. At last she felt sure that his kinsfolk had kissed him, and that she was forgotten. She went home to her mother, to the humble cottage where she lived. ⁋ Two days passed. The lord came to see whether she had found the leaves. "Thou hast come home, young woman," said he. "Yes," quoth she; & she put her hand into a box and drew forth the Leaves. The lord knew them as soon as he saw them. ⁋ Now there was a great reward offered to whomsoever should find these Leaves; but this poor girl knew nothing about it. The lord wanted the money for his own daughter. But he did not know how to get rid of this poor girl. He invited her to come to his mansion to take tea, and her poor mother expected that she would return home with much money. ℂ Now this lord wanted to take her life. So he lodged her in a fine room with a bed to herself. Above her head was a sort of canopy set with iron spikes, which was to fall upon her and kill her while she slept. When this canopy descended it was to make a great clang, so that the lord might know that she was killed. ℂ Lo! it is midnight now. The clock struck the hour. It awoke the girl. She saw this canopy descending closer and closer upon her. She bethought her of the *Leaves that hung but never grew*. And when she bethought her of the Leaves, she bethought her of the young man. She drew a leaf from her pocket, & immediately he stood before her. She sprang up and gave him her hand. ℂ The young man told her to will them all to sleep. She willed them to sleep. "Now then," quoth he, "let us be gone." He went to the door and opened it softly. The two stole away, and no-one beheld them go. All was still. ℂ "I am afraid to live with my mother," quoth she to him; "I want to go farther afield, so that the lord cannot find me." "So be it!" said the young gentleman, "I will accompany thee, go where thou wilt." ℂ He took her to his own home. "And now, at last," quoth the young gentleman, "we have a place where we can talk undisturbed. Shall we two wed?" She gave him her hand. "That is the very thing I myself desire," said the young woman; "I had thought to ask thee." ℂ The gentleman told the coachman to harness the horse to the carriage, and they both drove off to London. In London they were married. Then they came back again to Wales. They kept a mill beside the sea and lived there happily from that day to this. ℂ And I deserve a big pudding for telling thee this lie.

TWOPENCE HALFPENNY.

THERE WERE THREE BROTHERS and the three were travelling along the road seeking for work. Night came upon them, and they knew not where to go to find a lodging. It was dark, and the road they were on led through a forest. ⁋ At last they saw a glimmer of light, and they came to a cottage. The door stood open. They saw a table with supper spread upon it. "Go in!" quoth the eldest brother. "No, I wont," said the second, "go in thyself!" "Not I, in faith!" "Ye are fools, the pair of you," quoth Jack. And in he went, and sat down at the table and ate his bellyful. The other two watched him; they were afraid to enter the house. But at length they too went in and sat down and ate. ⁋ Lo and behold! a little old woman appears to them. "I have seen no man here for years," quoth she. "Whence came ye hither?" "It is work we are seeking." "I will find work for you to-morrow." They went to bed. ⁋ In the morning they arose betimes, and on the fire was a great pot of porridge and milk. And that was what they ate. ⁋ And now the old woman tells the eldest brother to fetch the tools from the barn, and to go to the forest to fell trees. He took off his coat. And here he is working hard! Up came a little old man and asked him who had bidden him fell the forest. He could not see this little dwarf, he was so small. Then he looked under his feet and saw him in the grass. (He was a tiny little mannikin, thou must know—no bigger than Twopence Halfpenny.) The old man struck him and beat him until he bled, & left him there. ⁋ Now the serving-wench comes with his dinner. She went back and told the other two brothers to come and fetch him home. They brought him home and put him to bed. ⁋ In the morning the second brother went to the forest. The eldest brother told him it was a dwarf who had thrashed him. The second brother laughed him to scorn. And now he too sets off for the forest. He took off his coat to fell the trees. ℂ Lo! here is something asking who bade him cut down the trees. Well! he looked all around him: he could see nothing. And it was a long while before he caught sight of the dwarf. Then he saw him in the grass. "Begone!" quoth he. The little stranger beat him to a jelly. ℂ The girl came with his dinner. He ate his fill: and the girl went back and told the two brothers to come and carry him home. They went down to the forest and brought him home. Jack laughed at them. "To-morrow I will go down myself," quoth he. ℂ In the morning he went down to the forest. And here he is felling trees! He heard something. He looked beneath his feet, and saw the little dwarf in the grass. Jack gave him a kick. "Thou hadst better keep quiet," quoth the dwarf; and the little old man struck him. Down fell Jack, and the little old dwarf well-nigh murdered him. ℂ And Jack was lying there when the girl came with his dinner. Back she went. She told the two brothers to come and fetch him home. The two went down for him. "No," quoth Jack, "leave me here and go away." The two brothers returned home. ℂ Jack watched the dwarf, and saw the little old man creep under a big stone. Then he got up and went home and told his two brothers to go to the stable and bring the horses out—all four of them. They took a stout rope, and the three went down to the forest with the horses and fastened the rope round the stone. They made the horses drag away the stone and underneath they found a well. ℂ "Go down, thou!" quoth the eldest brother. "Not I," quoth the second, "I wont go down." "I'll go down," said Jack. "Make yon rope fast and let me down; and when you hear me say 'Pull up!' pull me up; and when I say to you 'Let me down!' let me down." ℂ The two brothers made the rope firm and let him down. Down he went a very little way. The old dwarf thrashed him. "Pull me up!" ℂ Now he is descending again! He forgot the pass-word.

"Let me down!" He came into a beautiful country and saw the old dwarf. The old man talked with him. "Since thou art come into this land, Jack, I will tell thee something. Thou wilt find three castles. In the first lives a giant with two heads. And," said the old dwarf, "thou must fight with him. Choose the rusty sword. I will be there with thee." "I shall be afraid of him." "Go forward, and have no fear. I will be there with thee." ⁌ And now here is Jack at the castle. He knocked at the door. A serving-maid came to him and he asked where the master was. "He is in the castle; dost thou wish to see him?" "Yes," quoth Jack, "I want to fight with him." "He will kill thee." "Go, bid him come out." The girl went & bade him come out. ⁌ "Dost thou want something to eat?" asked the giant. "No," quoth Jack. "Come out, and I will fight with thee." "Come here and choose thy sword!" Jack chose the rusty old sword. "Why dost thou choose that rusty old sword? Take a bright one!" "Not I! this one will do for me." ⁌ The two take their stand before the door. Off went one head. "Spare my life, Jack, and I will give thee all my money." "No." He struck off the other head: he killed him. And this was the Copper Castle—so men called it. ⁌ And now Jack goes to the next, the Silver Castle: a giant with three heads lived there. Jack took the rusty sword & struck off two heads. "Do not kill me, Jack. Spare my life, and I will give thee the keys of the castle." "Not I," quoth Jack; and off went the third head. ⁌ And now Jack goes to the last, the Golden Castle. And the giant who lived there had four heads. "Hast thou come here to fight with me?" "Yes," quoth Jack. The giant bade him choose his sword, and he chose the rusty old sword. And they went out. Jack struck off three heads. "Do not kill me, Jack, and I will give thee my castle." "Yes, I will," quoth Jack, and off went the last head. ⁌ Now all the castles, and all the money, and the three fair ladies in all three castles were his. So off sets Jack, & the lady with him. He went back to the Silver Castle and fetched that lady. Then he went to the Copper Castle and got that lady. And the four went on and came to the spot where Jack had climbed down. ⁋ The old dwarf was there waiting for him. Jack sent the three ladies up to his two brothers who were at the top. And now the old dwarf wanted meat. Jack went back to the castle and cooked some meat for him. The old dwarf mounted a very little way. Then he stopped: he wanted meat. Jack gave him some meat. He went up a little higher. He stopped: he wanted meat. Jack gave him some. He went a little higher still. "Give me some meat." Jack had none: he had only a very small piece when he started. He knew not what to do. So he felt in his pocket and pulled out his knife, and cut a little flesh from his leg and gave it to the old dwarf. Jack reached the top. ⁋ His two brothers had gone off with two of the ladies, and left the third one behind. The eldest brother had taken the fairest lady, & the second brother had taken the second lady; and they had left the ugly one for Jack. ⁋ Jack asked her where they had gone. The lady told him, and he hastened after them. He overtook them by the church. They were going to be married. The fairest lady looked back at Jack. "That girl shall be mine," quoth he. ⁋ Jack took her & married her. He left the other lady for the eldest brother to marry. There was only the second brother now, and he took the ugly lady. So here are all three brothers and all three ladies! ⁋ And now they want to go down to the three castles. Jack spoke to the old man about taking them down. "I will carry you all down; but thou must give me food on the way." "All right!" quoth Jack, "I will give thee plenty of food." "Then I will take you down." And down he carried them all. ⁋ The old dwarf went off with Jack. Jack put one brother and one lady in the Copper Castle, & the other brother in the Silver Castle. And Jack himself went to the Golden Castle. And he kept the little old dwarf for the rest of his life. ⁋ There now! I have done.

THE THREE PRIESTS.

THERE WAS ONCE A PRIEST who went to dwell in a distant place, and a new priest came in his stead. And all the clergy of the neighbourhood came to visit the newcomer. And this priest had a manservant, and a wife, and one horse, and two cows. And whenever his fellow priests paid a visit to the newcomer there would be great merry-making. And they went on in this way for some years, until the parson began to suspect that his wife was growing too intimate with the three other priests. ⁌ So what did this parson do? He talked things over with his manservant. "Let me know when these three priests are on their way up here again, and I will hide in the wood." ⁌ And one day the manservant saw the three approaching. And he went to the parson and said: "Here they come!" "Now then!" quoth the parson to his man, "go into the house and ask for my wife, and say to her that thou wantest money. And if she enquire where I am, tell her that I have gone down to the town." The town was a mile away. ⁌ And now here are the three priests in the house! And here are great carryings-on with the parson's wife! Now wine is served and food in plenty. And there were high jinks while the husband was down in the town. ⁌ And lo! the servant goes to the parson in the wood & tells him everything—all about the three visitors within. "Now then!" quoth the master to the servant, "I will go down the hill and pretend to be coming up the road, and then she will see me." ⁌ And now he pretended to be coming up the road from the town. And his wife saw him approaching; and there were the three strange priests within his house! She did not know how she could manage to hide these three priests. "Creep into the great oven, all three of you," called the parson's wife to them. ⁌ By this time it was mid-day. And now the parson comes in. He feigned ignorance, and said naught to any one. And his dinner was brought to him. And his wife was blushing to her ears at the thought of the three who were hiding in the great oven. And he ate his dinner. And there in the oven were these three priests afraid to breathe. ℂ And now after finishing his dinner the husband says to his wife: "I am going to heat the oven to-day and bake some bread." If his wife was red before, she grew scarlet now. "Why art thou going to heat the oven to-day?" quoth she. "The sticks are still damp. I will get the man to gather plenty by to-morrow; they will be dry by then." "No, no, I will bake to-day. Go, lad, and fetch me two armfuls of straw." Off went the servant. ℂ And the wife perceived that she could do naught: the game was up. So she went into the parlour to sit down. "Be it so!" She was aghast. ℂ And here comes the servant with both arms full of straw. The parson takes the straw and opens the oven-door. And now the straw is thrust inside, and now the match is lit. And now there is a huge blaze. And he shuts the door. And now there is loud wailing! And so he burned them—those three priests. ℂ Then he began to wonder how he could get their bodies hidden in some distant spot. And as he was standing at the door, who should come up the road leading past the house but the chimney-sweep. "Here is the very man I want to see," quoth he. ℂ In comes the man, and he asks the parson whether he had a job for him. "Yes," said the master, "I have an old priest here who fell dead. I will put him in a sack, and give thee a sovereign to carry him away and throw him into the river." "All right, give him to me; I would throw in five of them for a sovereign." And straightway he took the sack upon his back, and down he went and threw it into the river. ℂ And now here is the sweep again! And when he returned the parson said to him: "That man came back again to the house after thou hadst thrown him into the water." The sweep was astounded. "Give him to me," quoth he, "I will settle the devil this time." ℭ Now this is the second time for the sweep. And he flung the dead man into the river, & hurled great stones on top of him, that the water might hold him down. ℭ And now the sweep is back again at the house! "That man has just returned," quoth the parson, "wet through. Here he is in the oven." The sweep was too enraged to speak. "Give me the devil at once; I want him this instant." ℭ The parson put him in a sack, and off goes the sweep with him. This was the last priest. And he flung him over the bridge & threw heaps of stones on top of him. "This time, old devil, I will watch thee," he muttered. And he smokes his pipe upon the bridge and watches him for a long while. ℭ Then he looked down the road, & presently he sees another priest coming along. But this one had no share in the guilt of the other three. "Now, thou devil, I have caught thee!" he cried. And so for no fault at all he flung the poor priest over the bridge. ℭ And now he went up to the house again. And the master paid him, and gave him plenty to eat and drink. ℭ And after that no more priests ever came to the house to pay court to the parson's wife. And the pair live there happily together to this very day. I was there myself, and I played the fiddle for them, and they gave me a great tankard of ale.

JACK AND HIS CUDGEL.

THERE WAS A COTTAGE and an old woman and her son. They were so miserably poor that the landlord had to come for the rent time after time. ℂ Now the old woman had three cows and naught besides. Said she to her son: "Let us sell the three cows at the fair to-morrow, that I may pay the rent." ℂ Jack set off with the cows. He met a man on the road. "Where art thou going with those cows?" asked he of Jack. "To the fair to sell them." "Sell them to me," quoth the man. "What wilt thou give me for them?" "A cudgel, a musical-box, and this little bee." ℂ Jack took them and returned home. "What didst thou get for the cows?" quoth his old mother to Jack. "These three things": Jack showed them to the old woman. "How foolishly hast thou acted!" quoth she; and she rated him soundly. ℂ Jack pulled out the musical-box, & made the old woman dance until she was too exhausted to stand. "Do but stop playing, my boy, and I will not scold thee ever again." ℂ On the morrow the landlord came for his rent. "I know what to do," quoth Jack. He called upon the cudgel: "Lay on, cudgel, lay on!" quoth he. The cudgel drubbed the man out of the house. ℂ Quoth Jack to his mother: "I am going to seek my fortune." Lo! he sets forth with the cudgel and the bee. He left the musical-box with his old mother. ℂ He walked for a long, long way. He saw a great castle, but it was only half built. Every day the workmen built it up, and every night it was demolished. The lord of the mansion had proclaimed that he would give his daughter to the man who should find out who pulled the castle down. ℂ Jack gathered together a heap of stones by his side, and lay down on the wall to watch the castle. He watched for a long time. ℂ Midnight arrived: it struck twelve. He saw two giants go up to the castle to pull it down, one on this side & the other on that side. ℂ Jack took a stone in his hand, and hurled it at one of the giants. "What art thou doing?" said this giant to the other. "I am doing naught." Jack hurled yet another stone, and hit one giant on the back. "Do not bump against me," said this giant to the other. "I did naught; why dost thou talk like that?" ℂ Now a great quarrel broke out between the two giants. They fell a-fighting, until they killed each other. Jack cut off the heads of the two giants, and carried one away with him to show to the lord. ℂ Now he hurries off to the mansion to tell the lord that he had found out who it was that had been pulling down the castle. He showed the head, & asked the lord for his daughter. ℂ The lord did not like to give his daughter to such a poor man. "There are three more things, Jack, for thee to do, before I give her to thee. To-morrow thou must catch the old witch who lives in the forest." He gave Jack plenty to eat and plenty to drink, and a good bed to sleep in. Jack slept all night. ℭ He rose early in the morning and took a two-handed auger with him to the wood. He bored a big hole in the tree with the auger, & waited close by until the witch should come. Soon he beheld her—a hideous old witch with long, long hair. ℭ She looked at the hole. She was surprised. "Who made this hole?" muttered she to herself. Jack came up. He bade the witch good-day. "What is that door in the tree?" she asked. "A pretty little house that I have made for thee; thou wilt be snug in that little house; neither snow nor frost will find thee there." ℭ The old witch came right up to the tree. Jack seized her hair in his hand, pulled it through the hole, and tied it round the tree. That was the way he caught her. He bound her arms and carried her to the mansion. He delivered her to the lord, and they put her in a cage outside the mansion. And there she was for years, spitting upon all the servant girls who passed. ℭ "Now then, Jack, I want thee to catch the wild boar, and to bring him to the mansion." "That is naught," quoth Jack, "I will do that for thee to-morrow." ℭ He went to bed and slept well. In the morning he arose, and took with him some victuals which gave forth a savoury smell. He laid the victuals beneath a tree. He climbed the tree to hide himself, and he had a big rope with him. ℭ The boar scented the savoury smell: presently Jack heard him galloping through the forest. The boar came right up to the tree. Lo! he is eating now. Jack threw the rope round his snout, and pulled it tight. "Well, here he is!" quoth Jack, "I have got him now." And he brought him home to the mansion. ℭ "I have still one more thing for thee to do, Jack," quoth the lord of the mansion. "Thou must descend into the lions' den: if the lions do not devour thee, thou shalt have my daughter." ℂ They flung Jack into the den, and he pulled out his cudgel. "Lay on, cudgel, lay on!" he cried. And the cudgel beat the lions to smithereens. ℂ All the people were dumbfounded; and Jack told them to lower a ladder for him. They were terrified of the cudgel, so they lowered the ladder. Jack climbed up, and let loose his bee. It stung the lord and all his fine friends who were there, until they were glad to beg for mercy. ℂ The lord saw that his daughter was to belong to Jack. So he gave her to him, and Jack married her. ℂ The two set off to visit his old mother. They came to the little cottage where the old woman lived. They knocked at the door: no one heard them. They knocked again: no one came to the door. Jack burst it open, and went in. There he saw his old mother lying on the flags. She had had no food in the house for days. Jack had sent her nothing, and she was dying of hunger. They summoned the doctor; he gave her a little brandy, and she soon came to herself. ℂ Jack took her with his bride to the castle that was half destroyed. He asked the lord of the mansion to let them live there. And the lord gave them the castle for their very own. And so far as I know, they are living there still, with the help of God. ℂ Ask me no more to tell thee any lies.

THE OLD SMITH.

THERE WAS AN OLD BLACKSMITH who lived on the hill with his wife and his mother-in-law. And the only work he could do was to make ploughshares. And the mother-in-law had an old mare. ⁊ One day there came to him a youth on horseback. "I want thee to shoe my horse." "I cannot," quoth the old smith. "Then give me thy tools and I will do it." ⁊ The boy went off and made a great fire. He came out and cut off the horse's four legs. He staunched the blood and put the four legs on the fire. He blew the fire a great while. He took the four legs out of the fire, put them on the anvil, beat them a long time, and threw them down. Then he picked them up, went out, and put them back under the horse. The old smith was watching him. The youth asked what he had to pay: he gave the smith a golden guinea. ⁊ Some days afterwards the smith remembered about his mother-in-law's mare. He wanted her shod. So away he went and brought her to the smithy. He tied her to the door, and cut off the four legs and let them bleed. But he did not know how to staunch the blood. He went in, made a great fire, and put the four legs on the fire. He blew & he blew. Then he went to look for the legs. There was nothing to be seen: he had burnt them all to ashes. He took the old mare and flung her over the hedge. ⁊ Now the mother-in-law and her daughter were always quarrelling. The old smith did not know what to do with them. In a day or two the youth on horseback returned with two old women. "Canst thou make these two old women young?" he asked. "No, I cannot." "Wilt lend me thy tools? I will do it." "Yes, take them." ⁊ The youth got off his horse; he flung down the two old women and bound them. He made a great fire, and put them on the fire. He blew and he blew beneath them. Then he took them outside, set them on the anvil, hammered them well and set them down. They became two young and beautiful ladies. The old smith was watching the youth. The boy gave him a golden guinea. ℂ A few days afterwards an idea came into the smith's head concerning his wife and his mother-in-law. He took the twain, and bound them, and set them on the fire. And he blew and he blew beneath them. Then he went to look for them. There was nothing to be seen. They were burnt to ashes. He flung down the hammer & went out. "I have done it now! I have killed my old mare, and I have killed my wife and my mother-in-law." He scratched his head and knew not what to do. ℂ So he leaves the smithy, and sets forth in deep snow and wind, with never a hat on his head. The young boy followed him & asked: "Shall I come with thee?" "No," quoth the smith, "thou hast naught to do with me." "Do let me come with thee." The old smith took him. The boy was barefoot. ℂ The boy talked to him. "Near by is a great castle, and in it is a mighty lord. He is ill in bed. Let us go there." "I can do nothing," quoth the smith. "Say naught then: we will go there together, and I will do everything. Tell them that I am thy servant." ℂ Down they went to the castle and knocked at the door. The butler came out. "We have come here to heal the great lord." "Come in!" He took them in to sit down by the fire. He asked them what they would have to eat and drink. They got plenty to eat and drink. The old smith forgot what they had to do. The little boy reminded him: "Now then, when the butler comes in, say that thou wishest to go up to the lord." ℂ They went up to the lord. The young boy called for a knife, a pot, water, and a spoon. He cut off the lord's head and spat on his hands to staunch the blood. He put the head in the pot, and set it on the fire to boil. It boiled a great while. He took a golden spoon & stirred it with the spoon. He took the head out of the pot and put it back on the lord's neck. The lord recovered & stood up. ℂ The lord gave them a sack of gold & they set off along the road. "All that I want," quoth the little boy, "is new shoes." "No, I have none to give thee: there is little enough for myself," quoth the smith. The little boy went off and left him. ℭ The old smith goes on alone. He met two men on horseback and they seized all his money. The smith journeyed on. He heard about a great castle, and how the lord of that place was ill. ℭ Up goes the smith to see him. The butler called him in and gave him plenty to eat. After he had done eating, the old smith went up to see the lord. He called for a pot and water and a spoon. He cut off the lord's head and let it bleed. But he did not know how to staunch the blood. He put the head in the pot on the fire to boil: it boiled a great while. He took the spoon and stirred it. He could do nothing to it: the head was falling to pieces and the lord was bleeding to death. ℭ Some one came & knocked at the door. The smith was afraid. "No one must come in here." "Wilt thou not admit the little bare-foot boy?" The old smith hearkened and opened the door, and the little boy came in. ℭ He walked straight up to the lord and staunched the blood. Then he went to the pot, took a golden spoon and stirred the head. It was a great while before he could get the head together again: it was boiled to rags. He took it out and set it on the lord's neck. The lord sat up. The smith & the little boy went away after getting two sacks of gold. ℭ On the road the boy begged: "I want shoes." "Very well," said the smith: "all the money is thine." The boy said: "I do not want it: I want shoes." The boy got his shoes. ℭ Now the two are walking along the road. The little boy said: "There is another great lord who lives hard by. This lord has a wizard & no one can beat him. Let us go there. There are three sacks of gold to be won if we beat him." ℭ They went up to the door to get speech with the lord. They were given food and came away. Then they went into an old house where there was a huge pair of bellows. The lord's wizard blew

up half the sea. "Now it is thy turn, little boy," said the smith.
The boy began to blow. He blew up a great fish that drank all
the sea. The wizard began to blow again. He blew up corn like
rain. The little boy tried & he conjured up birds that devoured
all the corn. The lord's man blew up many rabbits. The little
boy tried & he conjured up three greyhounds, & the greyhounds
devoured the rabbits. He beat the lord's wizard. They got three
sacks of gold. ℂ The old smith hardly knew what to do with
his money. It occurred to him to build a new smithy. And he
built a few new houses, a workshop, & three inns.   ℂ One day
he was doing a little work when an old woman came to the
door at nightfall to beg for a lodging. "All right," quoth the old
smith, "I can give thee a bed for one night. I have no servant-
maid, so go into the house, put the kettle on the fire, and make
some tea for thyself." The old woman ate something and went
to bed.   ℂ In the morning she arose; and she and the old smith
had breakfast together. "I will give thee three wishes: what dost
thou desire?" quoth the old woman. The smith said to her: "I
wish that the man who takes my hammer in his hand cannot
put it down again until I say so." He got his wish. "What is
thy second wish?" quoth the old woman. "Dost thou see that old
chair in the corner?" "Yes," quoth the old woman. "I wish that
the man who seats himself in it cannot get up again until I set
him free." "All right, thou shalt have thy desire." "And I wish
that the man who gets into my pocket cannot get out again
until I give him leave." "All right," quoth the old woman. She
thanked him and went her way. ℂ A few days after, when
his money had run low, a man came to the smithy. He asked
the smith how he was. "Very well," quoth he, "how art
thou?" They talked for some time until at last this man asked
the smith whether he would sell himself. The smith considered
a little. "Yes," quoth he, "how much money wilt thou give
me?" "I will give thee a sack of gold." "Give it me," quoth the

smith. "Thou must come away with me in five years' time: I will return here to fetch thee." The Evil One departed and the smith went out to the inn to get a drink. ⁋ One day he was in the smithy doing a little work, when the Evil One arrived. "Thy time is up, now!" "Very well," said the smith, "but wait a moment, take my hammer, and do a little beating for me on this anvil. I will come back when I have finished this small job." ⁋ The smith took his work home and afterwards went to the inn. He did some hard drinking there, came out, and went on to the next inn. He had a drop there too and came out. ⁋ Lo! the Evil One leaves the forge, hammer in hand, and goes to seek for the smith. He found him in the farthest inn drinking with the gentry. In came the old Devil. The smith stood up. "What art thou doing with my tools?" he asked. "Come here," quoth the Devil. "Remove this thing, and I will give thee five years more." The old smith took the hammer and went home. ⁋ The five years passed day by day. Just after they had come to an end the Devil walked into the smithy. "How art thou?" quoth he to the smith. "Very well! how art thou?" "Thy time is up, now!" "Very well! sit down in that old chair." The Devil sat down. "Wait there a moment," quoth the smith, "I want to go home with this piece of work." ⁋ The smith went off down to the inn. He got half drunk. The old Devil was tired of sitting down. He tried to get up, but could not. At last he walked off, trailing the chair behind him, down to the inn. He asked whether the landlord was in. "No," quoth the woman, "he is not here, he has gone on to the next inn." ⁋ The Devil followed him to the second inn, & strode into the parlour. And there he found the smith. He stared at the Devil: "What is that man doing with my chair?" said he. "Come here," quoth the Devil, "I want a word with thee. Remove this chair, and I will give thee five years more." The smith dragged away the chair, & the Devil departed. The smith returned home. ⬦ The five years passed day by day. Lo! the old Devil is back again. There was no one in the workshop: the smith was out drinking. The old Devil went to seek for him. He found him in the parlour. The old Devil sat down by him, and whispered in his ear. Said the smith: "I have called for ale. Turn thyself into a pound in my pocket that I may pay for it." The Devil did so. The old smith drank his fill and went home to bed. ⬦ He was just falling asleep when something under his head began to moan aloud. He got up, came downstairs, went into the smithy, took the pocket, held it on the anvil, seized the hammer & beat it soundly. "Let me go," quoth the old Devil, "and I will leave thee alone. I will never meddle with thee again if thou wilt release me this time." The old smith let him go. ⬦ Then the smith died, and he went to the Devil's door and knocked. One of the little demons came out. "Tell thy father that the smith is here." The little demon went and told his father. "Do not let him in," quoth the old Devil, "he will kill us all." "Here!" quoth the old Devil to his servingman, "take this wisp of straw and set fire to it to light him up to my dear God." ⬦ The Devil's servant did so. The old smith went up to my dear God. There he sits playing the harp, and there we shall all see him one day, if we do not go to the Devil instead. ⬦ And now that is all I have to say.

FROSTY.

AN OLD MAN WAS STROLLING along the road with his hat cocked on one side. His name was Frosty. He had walked half a mile, when he met another man. And this man was lying on his belly with his ear to the ground. ℂ "What art thou doing here, thou fool?" asked Frosty. "I am no fool: I am listening to the Members of Parliament making speeches in London." "Thou wilt be of use, come with me. Thou hast excellent hearing." ℂ The two walked on down the road. They met another man with a gun on his shoulder. "What art thou doing here?" "Dost thou not see what I am doing? There is a fly upon a rock in America: I am going to shoot it." "Thou wilt be of use, come with us." ℂ And the three went on until they met another man. "What art thou doing here?" asked Frosty. "There is a mill far away over yonder, and there is no wind: I am blowing the sails round." "Thou wilt be of use. Wilt thou come with us?" The man went with them. ℂ They walked along until they met another man carrying one of his legs under his arm. "Why dost thou do that?" "I have pulled my leg off lest I should run too fast." "Thou must certainly come with us." ℂ They went on, & presently saw another man carrying a huge tree upon his shoulder: a great powerful man was he. ℂ At last they came to a town. They heard the talk of the King's court—that he had an old witch who was a swift runner, and that a great reward was offered to whomsoever could beat her. "Let us go up to the palace," said Frosty. ℂ They went up to the palace, and Frosty and the King had a parley about the race. "I have a man who will run with her," said he. The whole band slept in the palace that night. ℂ They arose betimes. This was the morning on which Run-well and the witch were to have their race. They began to run. "Wait a bit, the old witch is beating him," exclaimed Shoot-well to Frosty. So he shot a dart into her knee, & Run-well beat the witch. ℭ The King was enraged at this. "Who are these men?" said he to himself. The old witch counselled the king: "To-morrow, proclaim that thou desirest the lake in front of the palace to be drained dry." The six were sleeping in the palace again that night, and Hear-well overheard this talk between the two. He told Frosty what was going to happen. ℭ They arose betimes. The King came and told them that he wanted the lake drained on the following morning. The day dawned; and out they went, every one of them. Frosty summoned Blow-well. Blow-well blew the lake dry; he blew all the mud & stones out of it and left it bare. ℭ The old King did not know how to deal with them. They had beaten the witch hollow. "I will lodge them in my old iron chamber and kindle a great fire beneath it until it is as hot as an oven, & I will burn them to death." ℭ Night fell. The old King summoned the six men, & threw open the door of this chamber. "Wouldst thou like to sleep here to-night, Frosty?" Frosty entered. "Yes, we will sleep here," he answered, "it seems a warm room." The old King smiled. "Yes, it is a warm room, & it will be warmer still presently." ℭ In went Frosty and his men. "We shall sleep snugly here." They sat down, and talked a little before settling to sleep. The room grew hotter and hotter. Presently it became too hot to stop in. So Frosty cocked his hat on the other side. The men were chilled to the bone, and began to shiver. When they were half dead with cold, Frosty tilted his hat up a very little. Then the room grew cool, and the six lay down and slept. ℭ The old King came in the morning to look for them. He was amazed to find them alive. He called them outside. "Go over there and get your breakfast," said he. When they had finished their meal, he returned and said: "I want a ship built upon that lake. I want to see it before the door to-morrow morning." ℭ Morning dawned, and the ship had been built.

"I want the ship to sail with no water beneath it." Frosty summoned Blow-well. He blew the ship out of sight, until none could see it. ℂ The King asked Frosty: "How much money dost thou want to be off?" "As much as one of my servants can carry." "Thou shalt have it," quoth the King. ℂ And here comes Strong-man with a huge sack! He opened the mouth of the sack. He half filled it. "That is as much as thou canst carry," said the King. Strong-man lifted the sack in his hand. "Dost thou call this trifle heavy? Fill it." The old King looked furiously at him. He filled the sack. "I have filled it now: there, take it and be off, and do ye never come here any more." They took the gold and departed. ℂ When they had gone the old King was beside himself with grief at the loss of all this treasure. He sent his soldiers after them. Hear-well heard them coming. "Wait a moment, I hear an army following us." The men halted & looked behind them. "Do not fear," said Frosty. The soldiers drew near to them. Frosty cocked his hat on one side. The soldiers were rooted to the spot: they were so benumbed with cold they could not stir. ℂ Then old Frosty paid off all his men. He went home alone to his native village, and bought a little house for himself. And there he lives to this day, and is flourishing. And the Woods went there and played the fiddle for him.

THERE WAS A LITTLE VILLAGE down in England,
and two brothers living there. They were as poor as poor
could be: they knew not what to do. ℂ They went to
seek for work, but no work could they find. Said one to the
other: "There is a little old woman who lives down yonder
in a small cave. Let us go thither. The old woman will tell us
whether there is good fortune before us." "Yes, let us go," replied
the other. ℂ They came to the little dwelling, and hallooed to
the old woman. The old woman knew that they were coming
and what they wanted. There was a great stone before the door.
The old woman bade them drag away the stone. They dragged
away the stone. "Carry me outside and set me on the stone, and
I will tell you everything." The old woman had neither arms
nor legs: thus had she been born. ℂ "Hearken both of you
to what I am going to tell you." Then quoth the armless one to
Jack: "Here is a little stone for thee." (It was no bigger than a
halfpenny.) "Keep this, and do not take it out of the handkerchief until thou comest to three roads." ℂ The two brothers
journeyed on. They reached these three cross-roads. They halted

and Jack pulled the stone out of the handkerchief. He looked at it. One side was yellow as gold and the other side black as coal. ℭ "What are we to do with this stone?" he asked of his brother. No sooner was the word uttered than he heard something whisper in his ear: "Spit upon it & toss it high in the air. If the stone fall at thy feet with the golden side uppermost, take the road on thy right hand; and if it fall with the black side uppermost, take the road on thy left hand." ℭ He tossed the stone high into the air, and it fell at his feet with the golden side uppermost. Jack said to his brother: "Thou art to take the road to the left, and I will take the road to the right." ℭ Now the two sat down and had a little talk together. "I go whither I go," quoth Jack. "Do thou remember to come here to these three cross-roads in a year and a day; and if thou arrive before me wait here for me, and if I arrive before thee I will wait for thee, if I be alive." ℭ They set off. It was a hot summer's day. Jack tramped mile after mile. He could see no house, and night set in. He walked all night until morning broke. Now he hears dogs barking: he stood still to listen again. ℭ He went on a little farther. He beheld a giant beside a tree, and heard a young woman weeping. She was crying out: "Stop, father! Leave me alone! do not treat me thus!" She was the giant's daughter. The giant was about to put a rope round her neck; he meant to hang her. The giant wished her to marry a certain man, but the young woman did not love him. ℭ What did Jack do? Jack took the stone & threw it, and struck the giant on the head and slew him. ℭ What said the young woman to Jack? "If thou bury my father somewhere in a secret place where none may find him, I will give thee as much gold as thou canst carry away with thee." "Good!" quoth Jack, "I will lay him where none shall find him." ℭ He was about to bury him, when he found the little stone in the giant's head. He heard something whisper in his ear: "Leave him where he is, and place the stone at his left

foot, and he will never be seen again." ❡ Now they both went
to the giant's house. The young woman opened a cupboard:
in it were a great many bags of gold. She gave one of them to
Jack, who put it on his shoulder & departed. ❡ Lo! he travels
now over lofty mountains until he reaches the sea. He was
weary, and the bag that he carried was heavy. He sat down and
slept for three or four hours. He awoke and saw a man coming
towards him with a great sack on his back. ❡ The man
came up to him. He recognized him. He stared at him. "Good
God, thou art my brother!" "Yes, I am thy brother, and I am
weary." He sat down and opened his great sack. "I am hungry.
See, I am going to eat!" "And I am hungry too," replied
Jack. "Why dost thou not eat, then?" quoth the other. "I have
naught to eat." "What is in thy sack?" "I have no food," said
Jack, "I have nothing but gold." "Then if thou hast gold, buy
thy food." "Gladly," quoth Jack, "give me my bellyful." "I will
give thee thy bellyful if thou give me a hatful of gold." Jack
opened the sack and filled his brother's hat with sovereigns. His
brother gave him a little bread and meat. ❡ The two fared on
together beside the sea-shore. They tramped for miles & miles.
They met no one; they grew hungry again. They sat down
to eat. Jack was obliged to give his brother another hatful of
gold before he would give him anything to eat. ❡ And thus
they went on until they rested again. They had not much food
left. The brother would not give Jack anything to eat. "Thou
hast got all my money," quoth poor Jack, "I have no more;
and if thou wilt not give me a morsel of food, I shall die of
hunger." "No, I have told thee, I will give thee nothing except
thou pay for it." "I have nothing left to give thee." "I will tell
thee what I will do with thee," quoth his brother. "Give me
one of thine eyes and I will give thee a little food." ❡ Jack
plucked out one of his eyes and gave it to him. His brother
gave him a little food. They finished their meal, and went on

their way again. ⸿ Another day passed; Jack grew hungry once more. He was afraid to ask his brother to give him something to eat. Jack grew hungrier and hungrier. He asked his brother to give him a morsel of food. "Not I," quoth the brother, "I have not much left. If thou wantest any more, pluck out thine other eye and give it me." He plucked out the other eye & gave it to his brother. His brother gave him a tiny morsel of food. ⸿ Poor Jack was blind now. The other brother took all the gold and left Jack alone. Jack knew not what to do. He crawled along on his hands & knees. He did not know whether it was day or whether it was night. He crept under a big tree. He did not care whether he lived or died. "If I am to die, I will die here." ⸿ Presently he heard creatures talking in the tree above his head. And who were they? A Squirrel and a Fox talking together. These two were in the habit of meeting here once a twelvemonth to tell each other the chief discoveries they had made during the year. ⸿ Said the Fox to the Squirrel: "There is a great city four miles on the other side of the mountain, and all the people there are dying of thirst. The water is dried up. And if they only knew it," continued the Fox, "were they to dig a well near the great clock they would find enough water to serve for three towns." ⸿ "And hast thou heard, thou old Goose-stealer, that the mayor of that place lost his sight last week?" "Not I," quoth the Fox, "I have heard naught of it." The Fox plucked a leaf. "Dost thou see this leaf, White-tail?" "Yes," quoth the Squirrel. "What fools the people of those parts are! If they were to rub his eyes with this leaf, he would recover his sight." ⸿ "Wait a moment, Sir Fox, I will tell thee something." "Let me hear it," quoth the Fox. "In the same town there is a princess with two horns growing out of her forehead." "Well?" quoth the Fox. "If they were to give her apples the horns would grow bigger, and if they were to give her oranges the horns would dwindle away. There is a reward

offered by the queen to whomsoever rids her of them." ⁋ And
this poor blind fellow beneath the tree was listening to everything they said. Then the Fox leaped down and the Squirrel
scampered after him. ⁋ Poor Jack arose and took a few leaves
and rubbed his eyes with them. As soon as he rubbed them, lo!
he recovered his sight. He was astounded. "Well! I will be off
to the city now." ⁋ He crossed the mountain and came to
the city. ⁋ Jack dressed himself up as a great doctor, and went
to the hall where the blind lord dwelt. He knocked at the door
and was invited inside. "I am a doctor come to restore the lord's
eyesight." ⁋ He went upstairs. There was the lord seated in
his easy-chair. Jack drew near to examine the lord's eyes. He
boiled the leaves & bottled them, dipped a feather in the bottle,
and passed it twice across the mayor's eyes. The lord regained
his sight. His spirits rose, he did not know how to reward the
doctor sufficiently. "What is thy fee, doctor?" quoth the mayor.
He gave Jack what he asked. ⁋ "Wait a moment," quoth
Jack, "there is one other thing I should like to do before I leave
the hall. I understand, my lord, that the water in your town
is dried up." "In truth, it is dried up." "Come with me, and
I will show thee where there is plenty of water." As soon as
the mayor heard him, he ran up to Jack and clasped him to
his breast. "If thou find water for us, I will give thee three
bags of gold pieces." ⁋ They went forth, and Jack led him
up to the town clock. "Seest thou this spot? Bring thy men
hither." "I will bring them at once." He brought them. "Now
then," quoth Jack, "dig down here." The men stripped for the
job. They dug down a little way. They found enough water to
serve for three towns. The mayor paid Jack, and Jack departed
with the reward. He shrugged his shoulders. "I am doing
well in this town, and I have still the king's daughter to deal
with." ⁋ Then he bought a basketful of apples and a basketful
of oranges, and set them down close by the gate of the palace.

He waited there for three days. On the third day the old king and queen & their daughter came forth in their chariot. And the girl had two horns growing out of her head. ⬤ The young lady cast her eye on the apples. "Stay, mother, look at those beautiful apples over yonder!" "Wouldst thou like a few of them, daughter?" "Yes," quoth the young lady. They bought a few. The young lady ate two or three that day. She arose in the morning. She looked in her mirror. The horns had grown bigger. The king's daughter was horrified. ⬤ Jack disguised himself again as a doctor, and went to visit her a day or two afterwards. "Welcome, doctor, I am rejoiced to see thee," quoth the princess. "Thou seest these horns on my forehead: dost thou know of aught that will reduce them?" "Yes," quoth Jack, "but thou must give me such and such a sum of money." "Thou shalt have it," quoth the young lady. ⬤ Jack pulled an orange out of his pocket, cut a slice from it with his knife and went up to the princess. "Open thy mouth, my lady, put out thy tongue." He placed the slice on the lady's tongue. "Swallow that. I will return to-morrow morning." The doctor took his leave. ⬤ Now it was morn. The young lady arose and looked in her mirror. Both horns seemed smaller. The doctor paid her another visit. The lady sprang up and gave him her hand. "The horns have shrunk a little, doctor." He gave her a slice of orange. "I shall come for my fee, your highness, in the morning." ⬤ She awoke in the morning and looked in her mirror. The horns had disappeared. The king and queen heard how the horns had been removed by this doctor. They gave him as much money as he could carry. ⬤ Jack took his money and went back to the three roads, where he was to meet his brother. It was midnight: he fell asleep under the hedge. In the morning he saw his brother approaching. "Who comes there?" cried he. "It is I," quoth his brother; "so thou art here before me, eh?" "What sort of luck hast thou had, my boy?"

"I have gained naught, I am destitute, I have lost all my money. And how didst *thou* reach here, being blind?" "I have had better luck than thou," quoth Jack, "I have got new eyes, and a bag of money twice as big as the one thou didst take when thou madest me blind." ⁋ So now the two brothers set off together to the cave to visit the old woman, the armless and legless one. They found her, and rewarded her with a few gold pieces. And the two brothers went to their own little village and built a new house there. And there they live together with a little maid-servant, and now they never fall out with one another. ⁋ That is all I know about those two brothers. Find out more for yourselves if ye wish!

THE EIGHTEEN RABBITS.

IN A LITTLE HOUSE ON THE HILL lived a little old woman and her three sons. One son was a fool: he was the youngest brother. ℂ Quoth the eldest brother to his mother one day: "I am doing nothing here; I must go and seek my fortune. Make me a cake." "Which wilt thou have," asked the old woman, "a big cake with a curse in it, or a little cake with a blessing in it?" "Make me a big cake with a curse in it." ℂ The old woman made the cake. The son took the cake and went away, and he was on the road a long while. At last he found a great gate and a fine drive leading to a mansion. He opened the gate and went up the drive. ℂ He went to the mansion & knocked at the door. Now the old master comes out. "What dost thou want?" "I want something to do." "What canst thou do?" quoth the master. "I can do anything." "Go round to the other door. Open it, go in and get something to eat." And he went in and sat down. ℂ Now the cook comes into the room. She asked him: "Wouldst thou like some ale?" "Yes," quoth he. The cook came back with a great tankard of ale, and plenty of bread and meat and mustard. He was hungry; he ate like a pig. ℂ And now the old master comes in and has a talk with him. "I have eighteen rabbits. And I want thee to look after them and not to lose a single one. To-morrow thou must go with them down to the fields." ℂ In the morning the lad had his breakfast and went out. The old master came to him. "Come here that I may speak to thee." He blew a silver whistle. Lo! the rabbits ran up to him. "There they are! and—dost thou see those fields down yonder?—stay there until thou hast had thy dinner, and come home at such and such a time. There are eighteen of them. An thou bring not back the full number, thy head shall be cut off." ℂ Now here is the lad setting off with the rabbits! He came to the fields, and found a little well. He sat down beside it. He put his basket down & the rabbits strayed, one hither and another thither. He sat down to smoke his pipe, and when he had done smoking he thought he would have something to eat. He opened the basket. Now he was just beginning his dinner when a little old woman appeared to him. "Give me a morsel," quoth the old woman. "Not I, indeed! I have none to spare; there is little enough for myself." So the old woman went away. ⁋ Now night came on. He had to take the rabbits back to the mansion. He got up, and went to seek for them but he only found two or three. So he scratched his head; and when he returned to the mansion there were only two or three rabbits with him. ⁋ The old master came out. He counted the rabbits. He saw that half of them were not there. The old master went back into the mansion and the lad waited without. The master brought out a carving-knife and cut the lad's head off, and set it on the gate. ⁋ Now I will return to my two other brothers. ⁋ The second son said to his mother: "I will go to seek my fortune. I know that my brother is prospering somewhere. Make me a cake, mother." "Which wilt thou choose? Wilt thou have a big cake with a curse in it, or a little cake with a blessing in it?" "I will have the big cake, mother." ⁋ Now he sets out on the road, and he comes to the same great gate and looks up. And there he saw his brother's head. He opened the gate and passed through and came to the castle. And everything that had happened to the eldest brother happened also to him. The old master brought a carving-knife, cut his head off, carried it down to the gate, and set it on the other post. And lo and behold! there are now two heads on the two gate-posts, one on this side and one on that. ⁋ Now I will return to the cottage. And there was my poor mother sitting down. And my brother was out gathering a little wood for his mother. ⁋ And now he said to his mother that he too wanted to go and seek his fortune. "I know that both my brothers are getting a good living somewhere. Make me a cake, mother." "Where wouldst thou go, boy? Stop at home! If thou goest on the road, there will be no one at home to fetch a little wood, or do aught else for me." "Make me a cake." "Which wilt thou have, the big cake with a curse in it, or the little cake with a blessing in it?" "I will have the little one with the blessing, mother." "Go, get me some water in yon sieve." ℭ Jack took the sieve and went to the spring, and there a little red bird appeared to him. The little robin told Jack to put leaves and clay in the sieve. And he did so, and filled the sieve full of water, and went back to the house with it for his mother. ℭ Lo! here is the mother baking the little cake. She finished it. "I know not why thou desirest to go away & leave me here alone." "I must go, mother. What should I do here? My two brothers have gone: I will go too." ℭ He journeyed along the road till he was tired. At last he reached the same gate. He looked up & saw the heads of his two brothers stuck on the gate-posts. For a long time he stood laughing and mocking at them, saying: "What are ye doing there, ye two fools?" And he threw stones at them. Then he opened the gate and walked up the drive. He was barefoot and bareheaded. ℭ Now he reaches the mansion. And the old master and the old mistress and the young mistress were all three sitting at the window. And the young lady gazed upon this man who was coming up the drive & smiled at him. ℭ He came up to the door, and the old master went out to him. "What dost thou want?" "How do I know? Anything thou wilt give me." "What work canst thou do?" "I can do anything." The master sent him to the back door, called him in and bade him sit down. He asked him whether he wanted any supper. "I do," quoth Jack. They brought him plenty to eat and plenty to drink. The old master kept on talking to him. Then he went away and brought some clothes for him, and told him to go & wash and shave himself.

"Put these clothes on when thou hast done." The lad went and washed and shaved, and undressed himself and clad himself in the new garments. ⟨ Then he took a walk round the place. The old master came out and had a talk with him. After they had done talking, the master went to fetch the rabbits to show them to Jack, that he might count them and know how many there were. Quoth the master: "Go down with them to-morrow into yonder fields. Do not lose a single one. I have their tally here in my book." ⟨ Morning came. The old master was out calling the rabbits. He blew on his silver whistle, and the rabbits all came to his feet. "Here they are, Jack! Yonder is thy dinner. Now be off, and come back at such and such a time." ⟨ Jack set off. And he came to the little well, and sat down. It was a summer's day, and it was hot. And the rabbits strayed hither and thither. Jack fell asleep. Presently he awoke to get something to eat. He opened the basket and was just beginning his dinner, when lo! a little old woman appeared to him. "Give me a morsel, Jack, I am hungry." "Very well, sit down and eat; there is plenty for thee." The old woman ate her bellyful. "Now, Jack, go whithersoever thou wilt, I will look after the rabbits. But come back a little before night-fall." ⟨ Jack went off to hunt for hedgehogs. He found a large one, killed it and skinned it. He made a fire, and cooked and ate it. ⟨ And now he comes back to the old woman. It was time for him to return to the mansion. The old woman gave Jack a silver whistle. "Blow this, Jack." Jack took it and blew. And as soon as he had blown it, lo! all the rabbits came to his feet. He counted them. They were all there. "Jack, bring a morsel of food for me to-morrow." "I will," quoth Jack. Then he went home with the rabbits. ⟨ Now the three come out, and the old master counted the rabbits to see if they were all there. "Yes," quoth the old master, "they are all here. Go into the house, Jack, and get thy supper." The old master talked with his wife. "This fellow will do for us." "Yes," quoth the lady. And Jack went in to get his supper. The three of them talked about him. "Wilt thou go again in the morning, Jack?" "Yes," quoth Jack, "I will." ⟨ In the morning Jack got up betimes to clean their boots. The old master also rose and went out. "Hast thou had thy breakfast, Jack?" "No, not yet." "Go and get it. I want thee to go down with the rabbits." "Yes, I will go now." "Thy dinner is in the basket, Jack." ⟨ The master blew the silver whistle and the rabbits came to his feet. "Are they all here?" asked Jack. "Count them," quoth the master to Jack. Jack counted them. "Yes, sir, they are all here." ⟨ He set off for the fields with the rabbits. And there was the little old woman sitting down. Jack gave the basket to the old woman. "There is plenty of food in the basket; I want very little," quoth Jack. "Now, Jack, go whithersoever thou wilt. But come back a little before nightfall." ⟨ Jack wandered a long way through the fields until he was tired. And now he comes back to the old woman. "Art thou hungry, Jack?" asked she. "No," quoth Jack; "there is food in the basket, if thou shouldst want some." ⟨ Then the old woman said to Jack: "Thou wilt meet the young lady on the road, and she will desire to speak to thee. That girl shall be thy wife, Jack. Bring me a morsel of food; do not forget me." Jack blew the silver whistle, and all the rabbits came. There was not one missing. ⟨ Now Jack was returning home, and had gone a very little way along the road, when he met the young lady with the cows. And Jack made his bow to her. The lady smiled upon him. The two had a talk together, and arranged to get married. "Jack, do not tell my father. I do not wish him to know. We will go away to the great city to be married, thou and I. We will set out in a few days. I will go first, and thou shalt follow me." ⟨ Now the lady set out for the great city, and told Jack where to meet her. Jack followed, and found the lady in the great city at the appointed place. On the morrow they were married in a big church, and away they went to a grand inn. They returned home, and after they had arrived Jack took off his fine clothes. And he went into the stable, and she into the mansion, and he groomed the horses. And the old master asked the young lady: "Where hast thou been?" "I was not far away," answered his daughter. ℭ Jack remembered about the little old woman and he went into the house to get some food to give her. "I will not forget thee." And he gave her the food. The old woman told his fortune: "By and by the old mistress & the old master will die, then thou shalt have the place. And I must have a morsel of food whenever I come to the mansion." "Yes," quoth Jack, "thou shalt have some as long as thou livest." ℭ They lived a year in the mansion after Jack had been married. And Jack was still a servant in the place, and slept in the stable. ℭ And now the old master and the old mistress died, and Jack got the mansion. He went to fetch his old mother. She was too old to live alone, so he brought her home to his house. He took her to the maid-servants that they might wash her, and his lady gave her new clothes. They led her into the parlour, & her daughter-in-law talked with the old woman, and was glad to see her there. She stopped with them until she died. ℭ And Jack & his wife lived there for years until they grew old. Then Jack and his wife died, and now their son lives in the mansion. ℭ That is all I have to tell thee.

THE ENCHANTED CASTLE.

THERE WERE TWO BROTHERS. One was rich and lived in a big house, and the other was poor and went a-begging. His wife had died years ago, and he was a widower and had one son. And he saw that it was useless for him to go begging from his rich brother. ℂ So one day he bought a new box for sowing corn, and he went up to his brother's farm with the box. "Here, brother, here is a new seed-box for thee, that thou mayest sow thy corn." "No, no, to each his own belongings!" quoth the rich brother. "Be off with thee, I will not take it." ℂ The next day he bought a long hay-rope. And he went up to his brother's farm, taking the new rope with him. "Here, brother, here is a new rope for thee, that thou mayest lead thy hay." "To each his own belongings! Be off with thee, I will not take it." ℂ And now the poor brother blackened this rope, and blackened his face all over; he was enough to frighten the devil himself. And at midnight he and his son went up to the farm. He took this long rope with him, fixed one end firmly in the ground and threw the other over the house. Then said he to his son: "Now I will go to the back of the house, and I will pull myself up by the rope. And I will climb down where the smoke comes up. And when I have landed safely in the house, I will pull the rope twice as a signal for thee. And do thou pay out the rope after me." ℂ So when he was safe within the kitchen, the boy unfastened his end of the rope, and up it curled, and then down into the house. And the poor brother tied the rope round his waist, so that it looked like a long tail. And he seized the two finest hams that were hanging in the kitchen. ℂ And the housekeeper heard a noise downstairs, and went to tell her master. "Noise!" quoth the master, "there cannot be any noise in this house." "Yes, indeed," quoth the housekeeper, "there is the noise again downstairs." He got up now to see, and lit the candle, and went downstairs with the wench behind him. ⁋ And when he saw what confronted him, his hair lifted his hat from his head, and a cold shudder passed through him. And he muttered to the housekeeper: "Aye! it is the devil!" ⁋ "Here," quoth his younger brother, "take these two hams." And the elder said in a timid voice: "No, to each of you your own belongings. I will not take them: be off with thee." "Open the door," whispered the elder brother to the housekeeper. And when the door was opened the younger made off. But the chilly fear did not leave his elder brother. He saw the big black tail trailing behind. "Children, children, see what a long tail he has! My dear God has surely been with us this night and stayed the Devil from devouring us on the spot." ⁋ Let us leave the elder brother now & accompany Jack. ⁋ The younger brother went down to his own home with the two fine hams. And he said to his son: "I have enough for thee now until I return. I am going to seek work elsewhere." ⁋ And he rose in the morning, ate his meal, & travelled afar to look for work. And he enquired about work from every one he met. And he saw a man approaching and enquired of him. "All who seek work in these parts go to the Black Enchanted Castle." "Indeed!" quoth Jack. But Jack had a stout heart, so up he went to the castle. ⁋ And he came to the great front door, and tapped at it gently. And lo! the lord himself came out to him. Jack doffed his hat and asked him whether he had any work. "Yes, I have work," quoth the lord; "to all who come here I give a week's work; and they fail to do it, and therefore I fail to pay them." "But I will do it, sir" said Jack. He led Jack in, and gave him plenty to eat and plenty to drink. ⁋ And in the morning after Jack had finished his meal the lord said to him: "Dost thou see this little watch? I have lost the small key; do thou find it for me." ⁋ And Jack touches his hat to him and starts on the quest. And he sought all day till he grew tired and was utterly heart-broken. And hard by stood a big old pig-trough full of water. By now Jack had given up searching for the small key: he was weary of searching. So he went up to this trough of water. And on the surface of the water there was a little twig about the size of thy finger. And he fell to playing with the twig, and thrust it down into the water. And every time he thrust this little twig down, it would bob up again. At last he grew tired, took the little twig in his hand & broke it. And as he broke it, the small key fell out of it. He was amazed. So now he runs to the lord with the key in his hand. ℂ "Well done, Jack! in faith thou art the best man that ever came here." There was nothing in the house too good for him. ℂ "Now, Jack," quoth the great lord, "thou must plant all this coltsfoot in the garden for me." And he gave him an armful of plants. And Jack went with them into the garden. He planted them all, but before he had finished the job, he found a rusty old ring. He did not know whether it was gold or silver, or what it was. He put it into his pocket. ℂ "Well now," quoth the great lord to Jack, "to-morrow thou must find *me*." And Jack touched his hat to him, and then went off to get his supper. ℂ And morning came. Now Jack begins his search. And he searched and he searched until nightfall. And he was out of temper and weary and heart-broken. And because of all these things he went into the stable to sit down. "Why did he not set me to search for a needle in the hay rather than search for him?" he muttered. And in the corner was a truss of hay, and there he caught sight of an egg. "I will suck this," said he, and picked up the egg. And he took a pebble in his hand to crack the top of the egg. And when he cracked the egg, the lord jumped out. "Good, in faith, good!" quoth he. And he slapped Jack on the back, and took him into the castle. ℂ So now Jack has got through the week's work. None of the others who had

come there had finished it. And there was nothing too good
for Jack in the castle. The lord paid him well and he went
home.   ℂ And there was his son at home and there was plenty
of ham left. And Jack took down one leg & made a good meal
that night. And thus they lived in comfort until all his money
was spent.   ℂ And a day or two afterwards he remembered
about the rusty ring he had found. So he went upstairs to get
his old waistcoat, and in the pocket was this ring. And he
pulled it out and looked at it. He did not know of what it was
fashioned—whether it was silver or gold. It looked tarnished
and old. And he cleaned it, and as he was cleaning it, lo! a lady
appears before him.   ℂ "What dost thou want of me?" Jack
was too astonished to answer. "I am the Maiden of the Black
Enchanted Castle, and that is my ring that thou didst find."
"Faith! I am a poor man, lady, and I should like to have plenty
of food." She gave him plenty to eat.   ℂ And one day he took
the ring out again and gave it a knock, but nothing appeared to
him. Then he began rubbing it. The lady appeared before him
again. "I should like," quoth he this time, "to have a beautiful
little hall of my own over yonder, and to buy up all the houses
that are hereabouts." No sooner was the word spoken than
the thing was done. And now his own brother—the wealthy
one—is a labourer in his service.   ℂ And he took the ring a
third time and rubbed it, and lo! the lady stands before him
again. "Faith," quoth he, "wouldst thou like to live here with
me in this mansion?" As soon as he spoke the word it was even
so. And they married with that same ring which Jack had found
in the garden of the Black Enchanted Castle.   ℂ And there
they live to this day, in prosperity, and all the great landlords
are their servants.   ℂ A big pudding for me for all this lying!

THE LITTLE CINDER-GIRL.

THERE WAS A SMALL HOUSE, & three daughters, and their mother. The two sisters thought themselves grand ladies, but as for the youngest, they used to hide her in the coal-hole so that no one would see her. They could not bear her, because she was so grimy. They were ashamed to see her about, and whenever any one visited the house they would say to her: "Be off, Little Cinder-girl, and hide thyself." ℭ The two sisters used to go to church. One Sunday after church they came home and began to talk about a prince whom they had seen there. The young girl overheard them. ℭ Sunday came round again. The two sisters went to church while the young one stopped at home alone. And a little old woman came to the door a-begging. The young girl bade her enter, and made her some tea. After she had finished, the old woman called the girl outside. ℂ There was a white pebble near the door. Said the old woman: "Take that white pebble and fling it against yonder rock. Thou wilt see a door there; open it, and go in. Thou wilt see a chamber; thou wilt see apparel; thou wilt see a pair of golden slippers. Robe thyself, come out, and pass on to the next place. Thou wilt see a little horse, lead him outside, mount him, and ride to the church. Do not go right inside, but sit by the door, and let thy horse be tethered near it. Come out before the rest. The young prince will follow thee; he will try to catch thee and to find out who thou art. Hurry home, restore the clothes to the place thou didst take them from, return, and say naught." ℂ For three weeks the young girl did as the old woman bade her. A grand lady entered the church, and there was nobody there who knew her. Every one kept staring at her, and the prince fell ill with longing to know who she was. He kept his eyes fixed upon her, and he followed her to see whether he could find out. But she had gone too far for him to discover who she was. ℂ And the last week the old woman said to the young girl: "Mark what thou shalt do now & do as I bid thee. Go to church, and this time thou must leave still earlier. The prince will follow thee. One slipper will drop from thy foot, and he will come after thee and find it." ℂ Everything fell out as the old woman had said. The girl returned, put back all her finery, and dressed herself in her old clothes. The two sisters came home and began to talk about the prince. And the young one was listening to them. She asked the two sisters whether she might go to church to see the prince. "No, thou dirty little pig, go and hide thyself." ℂ The prince wondered by what plan he could discover the lady. At last he prepared a great banquet and sent a proclamation throughout the land inviting all the young ladies to attend. The maidens had no idea what the prince wanted. ℂ The day arrived when the banquet was to be held. And here is the prince in the reception chamber! All the ladies came up to his chair. One lady sat down. The prince took the slipper and tried it on her foot. It did not fit: out she went! Another lady approached. It did not fit. He tried them all, and there was not one there whom the shoe would fit. The two sisters were there, and the eldest, who was yearning for the prince, chopped a piece off her foot: she would have given her life to get him. ℂ The prince asked: "Where are all the serving-maids?" One wench entered: she would not do. Then another girl: she would not do. Now the Little Cinder-girl comes in. The prince threw down the slipper. The young girl held out her foot. On went the slipper & the prince recognized her. The eldest sister would have slain her, had she not been afraid. ℂ Lo! there were great preparations for the marriage. The wedding-day arrived. They left the church and returned home. There was a great company of lords and ladies feasting in the castle. At last all was over and the guests departed. ℂ The pair lived together for a year and the lady was with child. She was put to bed and bore a daughter. The eldest sister was sent for to come up to the castle to look after her. She brought a puppy up to the lady's room; and she took away the babe and left the dog in bed beside her youngest sister. Then she took the child home & gave it to her mother. The prince saw the puppy and was horrified. But he said naught this time. ℂ The lady was with child again. She was put to bed and bore a son. The eldest sister was sent for to come up to the castle and look after her sister. Again the eldest sister brought a puppy with her. She put it in the bed and carried off the baby boy. She gave him to her mother. Then she returned to the castle to nurse her sister. ℂ The prince came home. He went up to see his wife.

The eldest sister was there. She lifted the blankets & drew forth the puppy. "Is it not a disgrace for a lady to give birth to a puppy?" The prince spoke never a word. He summoned his serving-men: "Get ye down and make ready to burn her." His wife implored him to spare her once more. "If it should happen thus again I will take what comes." The prince relented: the lady was set free. ⁋ A year or two afterwards the lady was with child again. She was put to bed and bore another son. The eldest sister was sent for to come up to the castle. She brought a puppy to the castle, put it in the bed, carried off the child, and sent him to her mother. ⁋ The eldest sister was looking after the youngest. The prince came up to see his wife. The eldest sister lifted the blankets, drew forth the puppy & showed it to the prince. "My God!" he exclaimed, "what a disgrace for a lady to give birth to a puppy!" The prince leapt to his feet in her bed-chamber. "Where are the men-servants?" They were summoned to drag her out of bed, and carry her down to be burnt. ⁋ Lo! the little old woman appears once more. The little old woman spoke to her. "Fear not, I am here. Thou shalt have thy children back again, all three." ⁋ The lady was to be burnt. She was carried out of doors. The prince came out of the castle, and he paused to consider what he should do. His heart was too tender towards his wife to watch her burn. So he went away, and left her to be burnt by his men-servants. ⁋ "Nay," quoth the lady, "ye cannot burn me; my dear God is good and he will watch over me." She kept a stout heart because of what the old woman had said to her. "Let her go!" said the old woman. She was set free. "Thou shalt become a young sow in the midst of the forest." As soon as the word was spoken the lady was transformed into a young sow. ⁋ The old woman told the young sow: "Thou wilt be slain; the prince and his court will hunt thee to death. They will cut out thy liver & hang it on the gate-post of the castle. Whoever takes it and repeats certain words will get whatever he desires. Fear not. Thou wilt be restored to life, and wilt recover thy husband and thy children." ⁋ She was in the forest for years, and then the prince's servants found her. They had seen her about for some days, and they went home to tell their master that there was a sow in the forest they had never seen before. "We will go and hunt for her. We will slay her to-morrow." The sow knew that the nobles & their train were after her. She hid herself. ⁋ Let us return to the children. Here are the three alone in the forest: the two elder sisters had turned them adrift when their grandmother died. The sow found them. She spoke to the children. "They are hunting me," quoth the sow, "and mean to slay me." Said the mother to her daughter, the eldest child: "When I am slain, go down to the castle and beg for a piece of my liver. Take the piece of liver & thou wilt get whatever thou desirest. I will return again to you. It was my eldest sister who caused all this trouble." ⁋ They found the sow and slew her. The prince told them to bring her liver to the castle. They took her liver, and it was hung up on the gate-post. ⁋ The girl went down to the river-side with her two little brothers. They sat down by the river. "Is not this a pleasant spot?" said the girl to her brother. "Would it were ours!" quoth the boy. "Well, I can get it. I am going down to the castle." "Do not stay long, sister." The girl went to the castle, as the sow had bidden her; for the sow had told the girl if she desired anything she was to go down to the castle to get a piece of the liver, and her wish would be granted. She went and got the liver. ⁋ Back she came. "Now then, brother, come here; I will show thee something. Wouldst thou like a cottage here?" "I would indeed, sister." She told her brother what the sow had said. As soon as the word was spoken, there stood the cottage. ⁋ The three went to live in the cottage. They were there for years. One day a stranger called to light his pipe, and stared at the three children. He knew not who they were. He

went down to the castle and told the prince about the cottage
and the three children. He told the prince that the three children
were girt with golden belts. The prince offered the man a
reward if he would bring the three belts to him. "I will go at
once." ⟨ He set off, reached the cottage and knocked at the
door. Out came the sister. The stranger asked for a light for
his pipe. "Come in," quoth the boy. "No," said the girl. "The
man will do no harm, sister, let him enter." ⟨ The stranger
came in and asked the younger boy to let him look at his
belt. "Nay, brother, do not take off thy belt." "Sister, the man
will do no harm." The man got the belt. He next asked the
elder boy. "Nay," said his sister, "do not take off thy belt." He
took it off and gave it to the stranger. He asked the girl for her
belt. "No," replied the girl, "I will never take off my belt." The
man went down to the castle and gave the two belts to the
prince. "I could not get the belt from the maiden, she would
not part with it." ⟨ As soon as the belts had been handed
over, the two boys were turned into swans upon the river. The
girl was left all alone now. Suddenly she remembered what the
sow had told her. In the morning she went down to the castle
to get a piece of the liver, and returned home with it. "May my
two brothers be restored to their former shapes!" As soon as
the word was spoken she recovered her two brothers. ⟨ One
day the sister was talking to the elder brother: "Oh, brother, if
only our mother were with us! We must try to get our mother
back." "Impossible," said the elder boy; "no, that is a thing
that cannot be done." "Indeed," quoth the girl, "I will get her
back again." ⟨ The girl went down to the river, taking the
liver with her. "I want my mother back again." Immediately
the word was spoken, she recovered her mother. The girl fell
down stupefied. ⟨ Together they went to the cottage and
the mother kissed her two sons. "How didst thou bring me
here?" she asked her daughter. "I will tell thee, mother. A young

sow came to me soon after thou wast slain. She told me to go to the castle and get a piece of liver." "That is so," said her mother. "Canst thou bring back thy father?" "Yes," quoth the girl, "I will bring him back." "When?" asked the mother. The girl went outside. "Where art thou going?" asked her mother. "I will return, I am not going far." ℂ The girl went to the river-side. "I wish my father to be restored to us." The word was spoken: there stood her father. He embraced his daughter, and hurried into the cottage. His wife was speechless with amazement. But she soon recovered her senses. Said the prince to his wife: "Let us go home to the castle!" ℂ "How didst thou contrive to bring me here?" asked her husband. "I will tell thee. Dost thou remember the liver which hung beside the castle gate?" "I do," said the prince. "Soon after I was slain, our daughter went to the castle to get a small piece of my liver, and when the word was spoken, lo! her wish was granted." ℂ The prince, his wife, and his children went down to the castle. They dwelt there for years, and the children grew up. Then the girl journeyed a long while in foreign lands in order to see the world. She came home: her father & mother were overjoyed to see her return. Both the parents died, and the children are living in the castle to this day. ℂ Well! those are all the adventures the children had. There is no more to tell. We have reached home with the help of God. And that is the end.

GOGGLE-EYES.

THERE WAS AN OLD WIDOW. She had three sons, and they lived in a little hut on the mountains. ⁋ On a day when a storm was raging and there was deep snow without, the old woman wanted a few sticks to make a good fire to bake her cakes. Only one little stick was left on the fire. "Go, one of you, and get me a few sticks." She begged and she begged. ⁋ At last the eldest son arose. He opened the door. He saw the deep snow and was dismayed and turned in again and shut the door. But after much persuasion he went. ⁋ Lo! here he is now in the forest. He gathered a few sticks here and a few there, until he had made up a small faggot. He walked on, and saw a lofty watch-tower among the trees. Never before in his life had he set eyes upon it. He crept round it to find out whether the tower had a door: it had no door. He saw one little window high up. ⁋ Lo! a huge head looks out. "Hi! young man, do something for an old gentleman. Fetch me a little water in that pitcher by yonder spring." "What wilt thou give me, Goggle-Eyes?" "Alack! I have nothing to give thee; I am very poor." "Then go and get it thyself, Goggle-Eyes." ⁋ He went back to pick up his faggot. Up leapt the sticks & drubbed him soundly. He fled home to his mother. He told her there were some cruel keepers in the wood. "They beat me, Mother, and would not let me bring home a few sticks." He took off his shoes and sat down by the fire. ⁋ Now the old woman asks the second son to get some wood. After much persuasion he went. He came to the forest. He gathered a few sticks here and a few there, until he came to this lofty watch-tower. ⁋ Lo! a huge head looks out of the window. "Hi! young man, bring me a little water in that pitcher by yonder spring." "What wilt thou give me, Goggle-Eyes?" quoth the second brother. "I have nothing to give thee, I am a poor man." "Then go and get it thyself, Goggle-Eyes." As it happened to his brother, so it happened to him. He fled home to his mother. ⁋ Now the youngest brother was a simpleton who sat in the ashes by the hearth. He got up and shook himself: he shook pounds of ashes from his coat. And he fell a-laughing at his two brothers. "It is my turn now!" ⁋ He went into the wood to gather sticks, and walked on until he came to the lofty castle. Out popped the huge head again. "Hi! young man, please fetch an old gentle-man a little water in that pitcher by yonder spring." ⁋ Jack went off and fetched him a pitcher of water. The old gentle-man lowered a rope to him through the window. He bade Jack fasten the pitcher to the rope. Jack did so, and the old gentleman drew it up through the window. ⁋ Now Jack happened to be gazing the other way, and when he looked round again there was no watch-tower to be seen. He heard a voice behind him: "Jack! Jack!" ⁋ He looked about him but saw no one. Then he looked down at his feet and there was a tiny dwarf hidden in the grass. "I am the King of the Forest, Jack. Thou hast broken my enchantment, and set me free." He felt in his pocket and gave Jack a ring. "Whatsoever thou wishest, rub the ring, and thou shalt have thy wish." Jack thanked him. ⁋ He put the ring in his pocket & went to look for the sticks. Lo! there were the sticks all gathered together, and he took them home to his mother. "This will make a good blaze," said the old woman, and she put the wood on the fire to bake her cakes. ⁋ Now there was a great castle hard by, and in this castle lived a young lady. Near the castle was a deep cave and at the far end of it a bag of gold, and at its mouth a fiery furnace. ⁋ It was proclaimed throughout the land that the lord of the castle would give his youngest daughter to the man who brought the bag of gold to him. All the youths of the countryside came to the spot, but the fire in front of the cave vanquished every one of them. ⁋ Quoth the eldest brother to his mother: "I am going to win the young lady, Mother." "Bless me, boy, don't talk so foolishly!" ℂ Now the eldest brother sets forth; but he was vanquished by the fire and returned home. ℂ And now the second brother ventures; but the fire beat him too, and home he came. ℂ "Well!" said Jack, "now it is my turn to go, Mother." The old woman laughed at him. "Do not be so foolish as to go to such a place." ℂ Jack set off, and he came to the cave where the furnace was. There was a crowd about the place, but none of them took any notice of Jack. Everyone knew he was a fool. Jack pulled out the ring and rubbed it. And lo! he went through the fire straight up to the bag of gold, and brought it out. ℂ The old lord of the castle was watching Jack. When he saw him pass unscathed through the fire he said to himself: "So he has met my brother, has he?" ℂ Then all the people went away, and the lord returned to his own room, and summoned his daughters. He asked them who the beggar-man was who had got the gold. None of them knew. The lord wanted to find out who this man could be. He sent his servants to enquire at all the cottages on the mountain-side. They could learn nothing about this man and they returned to the castle. ℂ Now Jack brings the bag of gold home to his mother, and flings it into a corner as if it were a sack of potatoes. He did not know what gold was, and his two brothers laughed at him. He rubbed the ring, and wished that his poor mother should have plenty to eat; and they got everything they called for. ℂ The lord of the castle was troubled about this thing. He searched for the man every day. And one day when he was out driving with his lady in the carriage he saw a cottage in the midst of the mountains. He drove home and on the morrow sent one of his serving-men to find out who lived in the cottage on the mountain-side. ℂ The serving-man arrived at the hut & knocked. And the old woman came to the door. "Who lives here?" quoth the man. "Myself and my three sons and no one else," she answered. The old woman was afraid of him. She feared that he had come there to turn them out of the house. The servant asked to see the boys. "Yes, sir, I will call them at once." She turned to the three and said: "There is a gentleman at the door who wishes to see the three of you." ⦅ The three brothers came to the door. The serving-man recognized Jack as soon as he saw him. He asked him a few questions, put his hand in his pocket, and gave him five shillings. ⦅ The servant went home, and told his old master that he had found the man. The lord sent the carriage and the servant to bring him back to the castle. When Jack saw the carriage, he laughed aloud. "What dost thou want with me?" said he. And he laughed again. "Thou must get into this carriage; my lord wishes to see thee at the castle." Jack got into the carriage and they drove at full speed to the castle. ⦅ The lord of the castle recognized him as soon as he saw him. All his daughters laughed at poor Jack and made fun of him. But their father paid no heed to them, and ordered the butler to bring Jack a tankard of ale. ⦅ The lord put a few questions to him, and all the time Jack's hand was in his pocket rubbing the ring. "Where dost thou live, Jack?" asked the lord. "I live on the mountain-side, my lord, with my two brothers and my mother." ⦅ Now the youngest lady kept throwing glances at Jack. Quoth Jack to himself: "I should like that young lady to come for a walk with me." After they had talked together for some time, Jack said: "I must go home to my mother now." The young girl arose and said to Jack: "I will show thee a shorter cut to thy house." ⦅ They talked to each other on the way. "What work dost thou do, Jack?" Jack laughed. "I do nothing except gather a few sticks for my poor mother." She showed him the footpath. "And now I must leave thee, Jack," quoth she. ⦅ Jack came home. "A lovely lady, mother, came to set me on the road from the castle." "*Thee!* My poor boy, have naught to do with a great lady like her." "Indeed, mother, I will have something to do with her, and I will bring her here into the bargain." ⓒ He remembered the ring, pulled it out of his pocket and rubbed it. "I should like to see the King of the Forest." As soon as the word was spoken, some one tapped him on the shoulder. "Here I am, Jack! what dost thou want?" "I should like to marry the youngest lady, the daughter of the lord of the castle." ⓒ "Very well, Jack!" quoth he; "what else dost thou want?" "I should like a large mansion near thee in the forest." As soon as the word was spoken, there was the mansion in the forest. ⓒ He rubbed the ring again & wished the young lady to drive up the hill to him in a carriage. As soon as he had uttered the wish he saw the carriage and pair coming, with the lady inside and two coachmen on the box. They drew up when they saw Jack, and stood still. The young lady stepped out of the carriage and held out her hand to Jack. Jack took her to his own mansion and they were married. ⓒ They lived happily from that day to this, and Jack became gamekeeper to his uncle-in-law. And he left the bag of gold behind for his poor mother and his brothers. ⓒ I got a big pudding for telling this lie.

THE MAN AND WOMAN WITH TOO MANY CHILDREN.

THERE WAS A LITTLE WOODEN HUT in the forest, and a man and his wife with a great many children. They were too poor to support their children. They used to keep them without food or clothes, and all the neighbours were annoyed, and declared it was a great disgrace. Now the man and his wife were afraid of the police, for they did not know how to provide for their children. ℂ And one day the man said to his wife: "Let us take them all into the middle of the forest and leave them there, and they will get lost!" But the eldest boy suspected something, and took a pocketful of rice with him. ℂ So they all set off, the husband and wife and children, & travelled through the forest a great distance. When they had gone a long way the father said: "Stop here, children, I will come back very soon." ℂ They stopped there a long while. But the eldest boy guessed that their father and mother had gone away & deserted them. "Come along, children," said he, "let us go home." And he looks for the rice which he had dropped from his pocket here and there on the path they came by. He sought and he sought: he found nothing. The birds had eaten every grain. ℂ "The children are too tiny to be told anything," quoth he, "they would not understand. There is naught for me to do but to find the way home." ℂ It was night and a dark night. There were a great many trees, and they kept knocking their heads against them on this side and that. In the morning they found their home. ℂ "Why! here they are back again!" quoth the husband to his wife. "Let us take them out once more," said their father. So they led the children still deeper into the forest. The eldest boy took a pocketful of peas, and dropped them here and there on the path they followed through the trees, until he had no more peas left. When they had gone a long, long way, their father said: "Stop there, children, I will come back presently." And the husband and wife went home, and left the children there. ℭ The eldest boy said to the younger children: "Come with me, little ones, let us go home." Now the eldest boy goes to look for the peas. There was not a single pea to be seen. The birds in the forest had eaten every one. "I am lost again," quoth he. He said nothing to the little children. ℭ It was night and a dark night, and they kept knocking their heads on this side and that. But soon morning came, and they found their way home. ℭ "Why! here they are again!" said the husband. "The police will come back and arrest me. Once more I must take them into the forest." ℭ The eldest boy cut himself a pocketful of paper shavings & dropped them on the path they were taking. They went right into the heart of the forest. The father said to his children: "Stop where ye are, we shall come back soon." ℭ The eldest boy goes to look for the paper and found it all on the path. "So I have tricked you at last, birds," quoth he, "ye cannot eat paper." They soon found their way home. ℭ Before the father reached the house, he saw little scraps of paper here and there, and perceived what his eldest boy had done. "Here they are once more!" quoth the father. He gave them some food and sent them to bed. "If they outwit me this time, I will not take them out again," quoth he to his wife. ℭ The next morning the father said to his eldest boy: "Come here, boy, stand still while I search thy pockets." He searched him: he found nothing. The eldest boy realized that his father had seen the strips of paper near the house. "Now then, I must watch him," muttered the father to himself. ℭ The husband and wife and the children set off once more for the forest. The eldest boy had nothing in his pocket this time. They travelled very, very far. "Stop here, children," said their father, "we shall come back soon, your mother and I." Both the husband & wife went home. ℭ "We have waited here a long while," said the eldest boy, "let us go home now." But this time the eldest boy had no trail: he was lost in the forest, and all his brothers & sisters with him.   ⟨ At mid-day they found a castle, and an ogre dwelt there. And the ogre looked at these children through the window: he thought them very tiny. He called them to him to enquire from the eldest who they were, and where they lived, and who were their father and mother.   ⟨ The eldest boy had a talk with this ogre, & the ogre questioned him. "I live in a wooden hut in a corner of the forest," answered the boy. "Come up here," said the ogre, "and I will give you food and drink."   ⟨ He took them upstairs where there were two beds, one in one corner and another in another. There were four children in the nearer bed, so he put the children he saw in the forest into the farther bed. The eldest boy overheard the ogre mutter to himself: "I will kill these children at once for my supper, and I will come back and slay the others later."   ⟨ He went downstairs, and had a smoke and a drink in his room. And after he had drunk and smoked he said to himself: "Faith! I am hungry now." So up he starts, takes a huge bludgeon and climbs upstairs. He clubbed the children in the nearer bed and slew them.   ⟨ The eldest boy saw all this. And as soon as the ogre had gone out, the lad arose and went to the other bed. And he lifted the dead children and put them into his own bed. He made his little brothers & sisters get up, and placed them in the bed where the four dead children had been.   ⟨ Now the ogre comes upstairs again, club in hand. He knew he had slain all the children who were in the nearer bed. So he went to the farther bed, and smote the dead children with his club: he did not perceive that the living ones were now in the other bed. "I have slain them now every one," quoth he. The ogre went downstairs.   ⟨ "Now, children," said the eldest boy, "get up and come with me, all of you." They crept downstairs and escaped. After the ogre had slain the other four children, the eldest boy noticed where he had put his club; and the lad carried it off with him. ⁋ Now here are all the children in the forest, & they want to go home. They wandered deeper and deeper into the forest, until they met a man. This man looked down at the little children & spoke to them. "Dost thou know," quoth the eldest boy, "the whereabouts of our wooden hut in the forest?" "Yes," quoth the man, "I know it, and your father and mother have gone off to such and such a town. Ye will never find them again." ⁋ The children wandered on and on until they came to a little village, and in this village they saw a constable. The constable gazed at them, five little children all by themselves. ⁋ And he went up to them, and asked them: "Where have ye come from?" "We have come from a little wooden hut in the forest." "Are your father and mother there now?" "No," said the eldest boy, "they have gone away to the great city." "Where didst thou get that club?" said the constable. "From the ogre in the castle." ⁋ This constable summoned three or four of his fellows, and they all inspected the club. "Yes," said one constable, "this is the spiked club of the ogre in the forest." They questioned the children as to which road they had taken. "The one leading out of the forest," said the eldest boy. ⁋ The constables banded together with a company of soldiers to go in search of this ogre in the forest. They found the castle; they found the ogre; they slew him. ⁋ And they kept the little children in the village, and built them a cottage, until they grew into big men and women. ⁋ A good hedgehog's liver for this great lie that I have told thee!

THERE WAS A BIG CASTLE and a lord and lady and three sons. And the two eldest sons hated their youngest brother. So the boy did not have his meals with them: he had his meals with the maids. He never got any new clothes: he got nothing except the old clothes which his two elder brothers used to give him. He was filthy. ℂ Now the old lady was heart-broken about her youngest son. "I know not what we shall do with the boy." "I will tell thee," said the old lord to his lady. "I will take out the three boys for a test to-morrow morning." ℂ Morning broke. The old lord summoned his three sons. He gave them a bow & arrows. The one who could shoot the farthest was to inherit the castle when the old lord died. ❡ The two elder brothers let fly their arrows. They shot far. Then it was the youngest brother's turn. He shot last, and outdid them both: he shot clean out of sight. The youngest brother won the castle. ❡ Now the youngest brother used to wander alone in the woods with his gun and a couple of dogs, shooting birds. One day he travelled so far that he grew weary. At last he saw a rock in front of him, and lying flat on this rock was his arrow. He was amazed to see this place: he had never been there before in his life. ❡ He walked round the rock, until he saw a handsome door. He knocked at the door. Out came a young lady. "Hast thou come to get thine arrow?" "Yes," quoth Jack. "Come in," said the young lady. He went into her room. The young lady made him sit down. She asked him what he would take to drink. "I will have a drop of beer." He got the beer. The two had a chat together. "Wouldst thou like to live here?" said the lady. "Yes," quoth he. ❡ She took him all over the place, & showed him everything that was in it. There were many rooms there & these rooms were full of fairies, little women and little men, beautifully dressed in an old-fashioned style. The lady told him to take no notice of them. "Do not stare at them too hard." ❡ Now this lady was the Queen of the Fairies. When she had shown him everything they both returned to her room, and the lady promised that he should be lord of them all. "Shall we wed?" she asked. "Certainly!" quoth he, "to-morrow!" ❡ The morrow came. "Go to the coachman, and bid him fetch the carriage and pair and bring it to the door." The carriage came to the door. ❡ The lady went to tell the fairies that she was going to be married. "To-day?" they asked. "Yes," quoth the lady; "go and array yourselves." ❡ So all the little men dressed themselves in their best clothes, red coats and white breeches and white stockings with buckles on their shoes. The lady told them to parade outside in couples, man & woman, in front of the door. Thus were they to march behind the carriage up to the church. "And now I am going to put on my own dress," quoth the lady. "And then we two will come out and lead the procession to church." ⓒ They went to church. They were married and came out. The fairies were to sing all the way back. They came home, and all the fairies returned to their own quarters. There was a grand banquet for them. They ate: they made an end of eating. ⓒ And the bride and bridegroom dined in their own room. The lady told her lord not to stare too hard at the fairies when they went in to see them. "I will remember," quoth her husband. They finished their meal, and went in to the fairies. "Did ye enjoy your banquet?" "Yes, indeed we did." After they had finished, they cleared the table and took the rest of the food into the pantry. ⓒ "I should like a ball," quoth the lady. All the fairies were delighted to hear about the ball. A fiddle was brought in, and one of the little men was to play. All the fairies stood up to dance a country measure. The lord and lady sat down to watch them. They liked seeing them dance. ⓒ One of the little men said to the Queen: "After we have done, ye two must dance likewise. We want to watch you." The lord and lady danced, & the fairies were all agog. They enjoyed watching the couple. ⓒ Then said the Queen: "I desire you to sing." They all stood up to sing. They sang well: they made an end of singing. "How dost thou like them?" enquired the bride of her husband. "They sang well," replied he. The concert was over, and all the fairies gave a hearty cheer. ⓒ The lord and lady returned to their own room. They chatted together. "Wouldst thou like to come and visit my father's house?" asked the lord. "Yes, I should," answered his bride. "Let us go there to-morrow, my lady." Night fell. They went up to bed: they slept together. ⓒ In the morning they arose. The lady bade

the coachman bring the carriage and pair to the door. It was
brought to the door. The couple came out, & away they drove
up the road. They went to his father's castle. ☙ And Jack's
two brothers came to the door to escort the lord and lady
inside. They both entered the hall, and in the inner chamber
were the old gentleman and the old lady. ☙ His mother did
not recognize Jack. "Who are they?" she asked. "Dost thou
not know him?" said the old gentleman to the old lady; "it
is thy youngest son." "Has he a wife?" "Yes," said the old
gentleman. "Who is she?" "I know not." The bride stepped
forward to kiss her mother-in-law. ☙ Now in this castle was
an old witch, and the lord went out to ask the witch who his
son's wife was. "The Queen of the Fairies." The witch told the
lord to ask the Fairy Bride to fetch him a handkerchief big
enough to cover his whole park. He asks her. She brings the
handkerchief. And it was so big, it made a tent for his whole
army. Said the old witch: "Ask the lady whether she has a
brother." "I will go & ask her at once." "Say thou wouldst like
to see her brother." ☙ He returned to the room to ask whether
the bride had a brother. "Yes," quoth she. "I should like to see
him." "It would be better for thee not to see him." "I should
like to see him." Quoth the lady: "Very well! thou *shalt* see
him." The young lord and lady remained there that night:
on the morrow they returned home. ☙ The bride told her
husband: "It would be better for thy father not to see my
brother." "If he wants to see him, he *must* see him." ☙ She
took a silver horn, and went outside with her husband. The
bride blew the horn, and her husband was sore afraid. ☙ On
the rock stood her brother. He descended, and asked his sister:
"What do ye want of me?" "The old gentleman up at the
castle wants to see thee." The carriage was brought, the two
brothers-in-law entered it, drove up to the castle and arrived at
the door. ☙ The bride's brother alighted & entered the room.

The old gentleman & lady were seated when he entered. "What do ye want with me?" he asked. The old gentleman made no reply: he was terrified. "What do ye want with me?" he repeated. He was a tiny little man, but he was strong and fierce, and he had an iron club in his hand. The old gentleman did not dare to speak a single word to him. ℂ So the brother flew into a rage. He smote the lord with his club and killed him. He killed everybody in the castle—the old lord, & the old lady, and the witch. ℂ "Now then!" said he to Jack, "here is a castle for thee and thy bride. Leave me in peace, and do not summon me ever again." Then they both returned home. ℂ His wife asked him: "Well! what did my brother do up yonder?" "He slew them all: it had been better for them never to have seen him." ℂ So the husband and wife gave the rock palace to the fairies, and went up to the castle. There they lived until they grew old. They died. They left the castle to their children: and the children are there now and flourishing.

THE BLACK LADY.

ONCE UPON A TIME there was a young girl, and she wanted to go to service. She got a place at an ancient castle. ⁌ And in this castle lived the old Black Lady. She showed the girl everything in the house, and warned her on peril of her life not to look through a certain window. And after she had shown her everything the Black Lady went her way. ⁌ The young girl was all alone. There was nothing for her to do about the house, so she read the books on the table. All at once she bethought her of the Black Lady's warning about the window. She sprang to her feet, and fetched a stool. She went to the window and looked through it. She saw the Black Lady playing cards with the Devil. Down fell the young girl terrified. ⁌ The Black Lady arose, opened the door and came out. She asked the girl: "What didst thou see in the room?" "I saw naught. Let me alone. I am weary of my life." The Black Lady beat her, and asked her again. "I saw naught. I will say naught. I am weary of my life." ⁌ The Black Lady departed, and the young woman ran away, and wandered bare-headed through the forest. She was weary & sat down. Just then a man came riding by: he was a gamekeeper. He asked the girl where she was going. She told him everything the Black Lady had done to her. ⁌ "Arise," said the man, "and jump up behind me on the horse's back." The young woman mounted, and they rode off to his mother's house. The man told his mother that he had found the maiden sitting in the forest. The old woman led her into the house, and she became their maid-servant. She was a handsome wench. ⁌ She had been there now for some years, and the young man had a mind to court her. He told his mother that he was in love with her. So this gamekeeper married her, and she had a child. ⁋ She was lying abed, when lo! the Black Lady appears. "What didst thou see through the window?" "I saw naught. I will say naught. Let me alone. I am weary of my life." The Black Lady seized the child and battered his head against the hearthstone. The Black Lady departed. ⁋ Now the gamekeeper comes home, and goes upstairs to his wife to have a look at the child. No child could he see in the bed. He asked her where her babe was. The young woman made no answer. The husband turned on his heel and made a great fire, intending to burn her alive. ⁋ The mother besought her son not to burn his wife. She had a great to-do with him. At last the son pardoned her, but he swore to his mother: "If it should happen so again, I will burn her." ⁋ Next year she bore another child. The Black Lady entered her bedchamber. "What didst thou see through the window?" "I saw naught. I will say naught. Let me alone. I am weary of my life." She took the child & dashed its brains out on the hearthstone. ⁋ Presently her husband came upstairs to seek her. He entered her chamber. He saw no child there. He saw the blood on the stone. "Thou hast killed thy child, hast thou?" The husband strode off in a rage, went outside and made a great fire to burn her. He returned to the room. He carried her down. ⁋ Just as he was about to put her on the flames, lo! the Black Lady appears. She asked: "What didst thou see through the window?" "I saw naught. I will say naught. Let me alone. I am weary of life." "Put her on the fire," cried the Lady. ⁋ As she neared the flames, the Black Lady cried: "Hold! bring the woman back. What didst thou see through the window?" "I saw naught. I will say naught. I am weary of life." ⁋ The Black Lady saw that she would reveal nothing. "Here are thy two children. And never again will I speak to thee, nor shalt thou be troubled by me any more." ⁋ The husband and wife live happily together and the two children prosper. ⁋ There is no more. Good night to thee!

THE MAID OF THE MILL.

THERE WAS A BIG MILL and an old miller and his wife and their daughter. The daughter was beautiful. The old people did not want her to marry. They wanted her to stay with them as long as they lived. ℂ And there was a young man who for two or three years had been in the habit of coming there to buy flour. One day the old folks went off to have a day's pleasuring together. The girl was left alone. ℂ The young man came and had a talk with the girl. "I have five barrels outside. Will they be in thy way if I leave them there for the night?" he asked. "No, they won't be in my way at all." Two or three words passed between them and he took himself off. ℂ Now night fell. The girl went upstairs. A suspicion crossed her mind about the man who brought the barrels. ℂ She looked through the window and she saw two men crawling out of the barrels. She locked herself in. She took her father's sword in her hand. There was a little window in the inner wall of her room. The man came upstairs. "Where art thou?" cried he. "Here I am. Put thy head through here." He thrust his head through the window. She struck off his head with the sword. ℂ He had a silver whistle round his neck. It fell down at the girl's feet. She picked it up and blew it. The other men heard the signal. Up came another robber. "Where art thou?" "Here I am. Put thy head through here." She struck off his head with the sword. ℂ She blew the whistle again. Up came another robber. She slew him. Up came the other two robbers, one by one. She slew them with the sword as she had slain their three brothers. Behold! five heads within the room and five dead robbers without. ℂ She blew the silver whistle again. Lo! another robber comes up. This one was the eldest brother. He thought that all his brethren were inside plundering the house. "Where art thou?" "Here I am. Put thy head through here." He did so. She struck at his head with the sword. She wounded him but did not kill him. Then he knew that his brothers had been slain. He was terrified & fled home. ⁋ Now morning broke. The two old people returned home. They were shocked to hear what had taken place in the house. "How did all this happen, daughter?" "Have patience, mother, and I will tell thee. Robbers came here to the house. I went upstairs to my own room with my father's sword in my hand. As they put their heads through the window I slew them, one by one." ⁋ Now I will pass on to the house of the robbers. Here is the eldest robber at home. He tells his mother about the Miller's Daughter. The old woman was infuriated to hear that her five sons had been slain. But they could not think how to get hold of the young woman. ⁋ "I will tell thee what thou must do," quoth the mother. "Disguise thyself with a false beard, and robe thyself in thy best attire, and pretend to be a grand gentleman when thou goest there to buy flour. Beware of doffing thy hat. Pretend to woo the young woman & bring her here." ⁋ The robber's head was healed now. He wore a silver plate to hide the wound made by the sword. He dressed himself in lordly apparel, donned a false beard, and went down to the mill. ⁋ Through the window the girl saw him approaching the house. She ran to her father. "Here comes a gentleman, father." "Who is he?" asked her father. "I do not know," quoth the girl. ⁋ The old miller came down to him. He gave him his hand. "How art thou, sir? Step in." He came in, and seated himself. He talked to the girl in a lover-like way. The girl lost her heart to him. He went home and told his mother. "I will soon bring her here, mother." ⁋ Down he went again. The girl saw him. She went out and gave him her hand. She was in love with him. The girl led him inside. The pair sat down and had a chat. "Wouldst thou like to visit my home?" "Yes, I should," quoth she. The girl went upstairs and dressed herself, and set out with him. ⟨ Now the two have reached the robbers' house. "Ah ha! I see thou hast got her, boy." "I have got her, aye, I have got her." ⟨ He took off his hat, and the young woman caught sight of his head. She recognized him. "Ah!" murmured the girl, "it is the Robber Chief." And she was sore afraid: she knew not where she was. ⟨ Now they placed the girl under lock and key. The mother and son discussed what should be done with her. "I will tell thee," said the son. "Dost know the old cauldron in the outhouse yonder, mother?" "Yes," quoth the old woman. "Make her bring the cauldron full of water and kindle a fire beneath it. We will boil her in the cauldron. Strip her ready, old woman, I will be there anon." ⟨ He strolled out with his gun to shoot rabbits. The old hag went and unlocked the door. "Come here, young woman, I want thee. Thou seest that cauldron, yonder?" "Yes," said the young woman. "Go and bring it full of water." She brought it full of water. "Kindle a fire beneath it." She kindled a fire beneath the cauldron. "That water is for thee to be boiled in. Strip off thy clothes and give them to me. My son will be here presently." ⟨ The old hag took away her clothes and locked the door upon her, leaving her naked. The young woman knew not what to do: she looked around her. She saw a tiny crack in the wall—the house was an old mud hovel. She seized an old poker. She went up to the mud wall and hammered at it with the poker. She made a hole that she could creep through, and she escaped. ⟨ Now the son came home. "Where is the young woman, mother?" "There she is, locked up." The son went and opened the door. He saw no one there. He went to his mother: "Devil take thee, mother! Why couldst thou not look after her?" ⟨ He called out his men. "The young woman has escaped, comrades, let us go in search of her." They took swords & guns and gave chase. ⟨ The girl heard them coming. She climbed into an oak-tree to hide herself. The robbers halted beneath the self-same tree. ℂ "Here is an oak, perhaps she is hiding in it," quoth the Robber Chief. He thrust his sword among the branches, and pricked her bare foot with it. A drop or two of blood fell upon his face. "Let us go home, my men, it is going to rain. It is growing too dark now, we will find her early in the morning." They went home. ℂ The young woman climbed down and hurried off. She crossed the hills, and towards dawn she struck the high road. She saw a cart coming. She was ashamed to show herself: she hid among the bracken. ℂ The cart approached her. She raised her head and looked at the man. She hailed him. The man pulled up, and stared at her. He recognized her. He was an old servant of her father's. ℂ "In the name of God, how camest thou here?" he asked. "I will tell thee another time; take me home, the Robber Chief is pursuing me. What hast thou in the cart?" "I have cases full of apples." "Hide me somewhere." "I have no hiding-place, young lady, unless I put thee in one of the cases underneath the apples." "If thou meet a man on horseback who enquires about me, say that thou hast not seen any naked woman." ℂ The man emptied a case, put her inside, and covered her over with apples. He whipped up his horse and they went on. Presently he espied a horseman afar off. "I see a man on horseback, young lady." "Say naught." ℂ The Robber Chief came up to the cart. "Where hast thou come from?" he asked. "I had to fetch apples from such and such a place." "Hast thou seen a young woman naked upon the road?" "No, I have seen naught." "I will search thy cart." "Search it an thou wilt." ℂ The Robber Chief leapt down, and went to the cart. There were three cases of apples in it. The driver was sitting on the case in which the girl was hiding. The robber opened one case. He found nothing but apples. He opened another. Still apples. He muttered to himself: "Nothing but apples there." He rode off to seek her elsewhere. "The Robber Chief has gone, young lady," quoth the carter. ⁋ The robber rode a great distance in search of her. He scoured the country for miles and miles, and at last caught the cart up again close to her home. It occurred to him that he had not searched the last case. He stopped the cart once more. The old man was sitting on the case. "Get up, I want to see what is inside." "There is nothing but apples," said the carter. He got up angrily and opened it. The robber turned over a few apples. "Do not bruise all my apples, I want to sell them." "No, she is not here," muttered the chief. He mounted his horse and rode off. "The Robber Chief has gone away again, young lady," quoth the carter; "have no fear, he will return no more." He whipped up his horse. ⁋ Presently they reached home. The man went into the house. He told the old lady that he had seen a naked woman by the high road hidden among the bracken. "Where is she?" quoth the old lady. "I have her in the cart; I hid her beneath the apples." "Here, take this blanket, wrap it round her, and bring her in." ⁋ The old lady looked at her and recognized her. "It is my child." She was carried upstairs and put to bed. The old lady questioned the man as to how it had come about. The carter told her all he knew, and everything he had seen. She thanked him again and again. There was nothing in the house good enough for the old lady to give him. ⁋ The old folk did not know what steps to take to catch the Robber Chief. "I will tell thee, wife, what must be done. Send hither and thither throughout the land to make known to all that a banquet will be held here, followed by a ball." ⁋ The feast is prepared, and all the young men in the neighbourhood have assembled. The Robber Chief was afraid to be present. The young woman came into the room to see whether he was there. The girl went to tell her father that the Robber Chief had not come. "Have patience, daughter, we will go to fetch him." ⁋ The old miller with three or four men went in a trap to fetch him. They reached the robber's

house & the miller entered. His men waited outside. The robber
stood up and shook hands with the old man. "Art thou coming
down to the old mill?" "No, I am not in a mood to come, I am
not well." "Come down, we will take thee: my trap is at the
door." ℂ He needed much persuasion before he would come.
At last he put on his hat and accompanied them. He arrived at
the house and entered the room. The Robber Chief kept his hat
on his head. All the gentlemen asked him: "Why dost thou not
take off thy hat?" "I never take off my hat." ℂ Now they are
all feasting. They ate and made an end. Every one had to make
a speech after the feast was over. The young woman entered
after all had said their say. Now it is the young woman's
turn to speak. The whole table was listening to the young
woman. ℂ "There was a young man who used to come here
for years to buy flour. Once he came in the afternoon with five
barrels. He left them under my window. Neither my father
nor my mother was at home; I was alone. His five brothers
were hiding in the barrels. Night fell. They crept out to rob
the house. The five brothers thrust their heads through my
window. I had my father's sword in my hand and I struck off
their heads, one after another. The eldest brother put his head
through the window last of all. I wounded him on the head,
but did not kill him." ℂ The Robber Chief was trembling
with fear. He said not a word. ℂ "He came here again in fine
apparel. He made love to me & invited me to accompany him
to his house. I did not recognize him: I went with him. They
locked me up in a room. The mother and her son made ready
to boil me in a cauldron. The old woman forced me to strip off
my clothes and left me locked up until her son returned. The
house was built of mud. I broke a way out for myself and fled
naked: I escaped. The robbers pursued me. I heard them, and
climbed a tree to hide myself. They came beneath the tree. The
Robber Chief thrust his sword among the branches: he pricked

my foot. A drop or two of blood fell upon his face. 'Let us go home, comrades, it is going to rain,' said he. They went home. I climbed down and ran away. I saw a cart and hid myself in the bracken. I hailed the carter. He knew me: he took me and hid me under some apples. Up came the Robber Chief on horseback. The robber asked the man whether he had seen a naked woman upon the road. 'No,' quoth the old carter, 'I have not seen any such thing.' The robber searched the cart. He did not find me. He searched a second time, but did not find me. The old carter brought me home. ℂ Behold the Robber Chief here in front of you! If ye believe me not, pull off his hat. Ye will see for yourselves a silver plate upon his head where I wounded him with my father's sword." ℂ "What shall we do with him?" asked the guests of one another. "Let us leave the decision to the eldest gentleman in our company." They all asked the old man: "What is to be his fate?" "He must be burnt to death," said the eldest gentleman. ℂ A huge fire was made, and the men bound him and carried him out, and flung him on the fire. All the guests stood round the fire warming themselves and laughing. ℂ The Robber Chief was burned to ashes. And nothing more will ever be heard about this Robber Chief.